How I Met
The Salvation Army

*True Stories of Christian
Transformation*

Crest Books

The Salvation Army National Publications
615 Slaters Lane
Alexandria, Virginia 22313

© The Salvation Army 2011
Published by Crest Books
The Salvation Army National Headquarters
615 Slaters Lane
Alexandria, VA 22313
Phone: 703/684-5523
Fax: 703/302-8617

Major Ed Forster, Editor in Chief and National Literary Secretary
Judith Brown, Crest Books Coordinator
Lisa Jones, Cover and Interior Design

Available from The Salvation Army Supplies and Purchasing Departments
    Des Plaines, IL – (847) 937-8896
    West Nyack, NY – (888) 488-4882
    Atlanta, GA – (800) 786-7372
    Long Beach, CA – (847) 937-8896

Also available at http://www.shop.salvationarmy.org

Printed in the United States of America

Library of Congress Control Number: 2011924401

ISBN: 978-0-9831482-2-7

Contents

Introduction

People come to The Salvation Army in all sorts of ways. Some come to volunteer, others join a Sunday school, some come in crisis—either to help or be helped. In some cases, friends and family members have been instrumental in inviting newcomers to a worship service, a women's ministry program or to men's club.

The 96 stories included in this book are all different, but they are all about spiritual transformation through involvement in Christian ministry. While each person came to the Army in their own unique way, they all had the similar experience of having people in The Salvation Army who took a personal interest in them.

In these pages you will read of a man who found a book about the Army's founder, William Booth, at a dump, and how he followed up his reading by searching for his local Salvation Army corps. He attended worship services, got involved in ministry outreach and eventually went into training to become an officer/minister in the Army.

Another of the stories is about a young girl who was ministered to in her mobile home park by a Salvationist woman who faithfully took her to Sunday school. There are also remarkable stories of people who came to know the Lord and the Army through its adult rehabilitation services.

One man says, "I came to the Army very late in life. I was 75 years old when I became a soldier in The Salvation Army." Another couple got involved while helping the Army distribute turkeys to people in need during Thanksgiving, while others came because of their connection to the Army's massive Christmas efforts.

As a first–generation Salvationist myself, the experience of others rings true with me. We each found a warm welcome and a challenging, purpose–driven, multi-faceted ministry that engaged us and helped transform our lives.

We pray that you will be inspired by these very personal stories, shared by the people who experienced them. We also pray that you will be further motivated in your desire to serve Jesus, and to help others in His name.

Major Ed Forster
Editor in Chief and National Literary Secretary

1 Outreach Ministry

"He said to them, 'Go into all the world
and preach the gospel to all creation.'"

Mark 16:15

A Fan of Veggie Tales
Lifts Up Her Voice

My name is Angel Arnold. I live in Decatur, Illinois and I attend The Salvation Army. I was born in Evanston, Illinois, a suburb near Chicago. I was active in a church. When I was around eight or nine years old, my mom decided to move us to Wheaton, Illinois where we stopped attending church for a while. During this time I fell in love with Veggie Tales. They told Bible stories in such a unique way.

Angel Arnold

Family On Track

We only stayed in Wheaton for ten months, then we moved to Aurora, Illinois where we picked up on church again. We started going to a Baptist church and that is where I met Jesus as my Savior and really started getting into the Word of God. I started to learn how to be more like Christ. It was also my responsibility and privilege to keep my family on a spiritual track. My family consisted of me, my mom, little sister and my grandmother.

I have always loved going to church, but at times I felt like I didn't fit in with the other children, though everyone knew me. That's where I began to sing and discovered a God–given talent. I used to sing a solo every Sunday. About a year or so later my mom, sister and I packed our bags and went to Decatur.

We didn't know anyone there and we didn't know what this little city was about.

Daily Walks

One hot summer day, just before I entered the fifth grade, my mom, sister and I started taking daily walks downtown. We took different routes each time in search of a church and something to keep us going. One day we saw a sign about two blocks from where we lived that announced that The Salvation Army was having Vacation Bible School and that the theme was Veggie Tales. Even though we had missed a couple of days, we still went that evening.

As soon as we walked through the doors we could definitely feel the love in this place of worship. Everyone greeted us as though we had known them forever, which felt weird, but we felt welcome. That evening Majors John and Carol Wilkins, corps officers at the time, and some of the leaders invited us to come to church on Sunday. We, as a family, weren't doing anything, and we were looking for a church home so we decided, why not? It was only two blocks away from where we lived.

Feeling the Love

That Sunday was great! I thought the love I felt at VBS was great, but the love I felt at church was even more abundant. It was a place filled with joy and with people who truly worshiped the Lord.

Later I became a Junior Soldier and now I am a Senior Soldier. A year ago I won first place in a solo contest at music camp, which made me start singing once again. This past summer I was able to be on the program staff at camp, so I was able to share God's love with many children.

Because of The Salvation Army, my sister is now a Junior Soldier and she just loves going to church and learning more about Christ.

Now when anyone asks me what church I attend, I proudly say, The Salvation Army! Come join our Army! There is a place for you!

Angel Arnold lives in Decatur, IL.

The Blue Station Wagon
An Officer Walked in My Neighborhood

Sitting on the front steps of our apartment complex, a friend and I were trying to figure out what we were going to do next; homework was finished and there was still plenty of time to play before dinner. It would turn out to be a day I will always remember. It changed not only my life but those of my mother and siblings as well.

All of a sudden, this big blue station wagon pulled up in front of the house. A short, white–haired man started walking

Ann L. Bennett

towards us. He was wearing the strangest looking outfit and a funny hat (that's what it looked like to a seven year–old).

Frightened, we quickly got up and ran inside.

Seconds later, there was a knock at the door. Mom told me to answer the door and there he was—he leaned over and put his hand out to shake mine. Mom was behind me and said it was okay. He introduced himself as Brigadier Hoffman from The Salvation Army.

The Visit

Dad arrived home from work as mom invited the brigadier in for a cup of coffee. The three sat in the kitchen talking about VBS (Vacation Bible School). We didn't know what VBS was, but my friend and I played near the kitchen entryway and listened as this man told the story of how my dad had himself attended VBS as a young boy.

Brigadier spoke of Sunday school, camp and things I didn't understand at that time. Dad explained that his family was Catholic and never went back to the Army; but periodic visits helped his parents during Thanksgiving and Christmas.

As the oldest of four, most of my time at home was spent staying out of trouble or doing what I could to help keep younger brothers busy while mom cared for the baby.

New Life for Our Family

From that day on, life changed. Early each Sunday morning the big blue station wagon showed up as transportation to Sunday school. Soon it was summertime and almost every day the wagon showed up for programs, VBS or camp. As each sibling became of age, they joined me. Spending time at the Army was fun.

Yes, the Army became my life—but more importantly, a new found life in Christ Jesus was what kept a young teenage girl like me out of trouble. A full range of Army–related youth activities were available for my family. And mom joined the Home League and stood at kettles at Christmas. There was always something new and exciting at our house thanks to the Army.

I thank God for the corps officer who thought it important enough to "reach out" some 25 plus years later and make contact with my family through a "home visit." Our lives were changed!

Last June, our territorial commander challenged newly commissioned Lieutenants to walk their neighborhoods surrounding their corps and quarters. Meeting new people and sharing the love of Jesus is a powerful experience. Home visits ... hummm?

Ann L. Bennett and her husband Ken are soldiers in the Seneca, SC corps.

The Nearness of God
A New Reality for Me

My mother was a hard working woman. She hardly spent time with me and my brother because she was the main provider for the household. My father couldn't hold a job. A lot of the time what my mother would bring home he would spend on alcohol, which greatly multiplied my mother's burdens through the years.

I had a very tough childhood, experiencing physical abuse due to my father's alcohol addiction. I never really had a connection with the Lord, because my

Lt. Lourdes Murillo

parents' God was a distant God, a God that had nothing to do with their lives and therefore would have nothing to do with ours. I grew up bitter toward God so that faith and hope were not part of my understanding.

As a result, my teenage years were chaotic. As a family we drifted far apart. Both of my parents were sick. My mom was dealing with a mental illness and my dad had been diagnosed with cancer.

At a time when the sky seemed to be falling on me it was hard to conceive, let alone understand, the words my grandmother had spoken to me when I was a child. She loved the Lord, and she had always taught us that if we'd call on Him, He would be there. I had done that numerous times, and I thought that nothing happened.

Unexpected

In May of 2003 I went to The Salvation Army with a friend, who had invited me over and over. To be honest, the last thing I expected was for God to reveal His love to me. On that day my eyes were opened and I saw God's love for the first time. Through His Word He told me: "I have loved you with everlasting love, therefore I have prolonged My mercy" (Jer. 31:3). That day I poured out my life to God. After having so much bitterness toward Him, I learned that His love was available for me too.

The officers at the Salvation Army corps took me under their wing, becoming my spiritual parents. They nurtured and helped me in my Christian development.

My parents' God was a distant God, a God that had nothing to do with their lives ...

I became active in the church, but God was asking more of me. In 2004, at a youth retreat, God began calling me into full time ministry.

In 2006, I entered the School For Officer Training through the prompting of the Holy Spirit. I was confident that He would be faithful to equip me for the ministry of saving souls in His name.

God has certainly blessed me. He provided salvation, love, a unique calling and wonderful people to love and who love me.

To my amazement, God has also provided a wonderful, godly man to work alongside me in ministry. God has certainly been good to me and I praise Him for His faithfulness.

Lieutenant Lourdes Murillo, ordained and commissioned as a Salvation Army officer in 2008, is now married to Captain Daniel Gomez.

Camper Comes Full Circle
Ex-Cop, Marine Renews Old Ties

Four children, two grandkids, six years in the Marines, 27 years as a cop and a wife of 38 years are the measures of one man's life changed by a summer experience at a Salvation Army Camp.

This past July, that same man, now Salvation Army Captain Ed Long, will help give 150 disadvantaged Baltimore area youngsters that same one–week experience at the very same camp that redirected his misguided childhood 46 years ago.

Captain Ed Long

"I was a very bad boy," proclaims Ed of his early teen years in Wheeling, West Virginia. "Let's just say I had some friends and we got into some things. Some not so good things."

Captain Ed, who now oversees The Salvation Army Middle River Boys and Girls Club, says that all changed after taking part in a few Boys Club activities at The Salvation Army's Wheeling, WV Corps Community Center, and an invitation to attend several summer residential camping sessions at The Salvation Army's Camp Tomahawk in Hedgesville, West Virginia.

Camp Fellowship

During his first summer stint as a boy, Ed fellowshipped with new–found friends under positive adult supervision while gaining a love for the great outdoors. He learned to swim, climb, boat and hike on Tomahawk's contemporary campgrounds and fostered his faith in God through ongoing Bible Study lessons and nature walks.

"Even as a kid, it didn't take long to realize that I was having more fun running, playing, learning and being good around people who were good for me, than stirring up trouble in the streets at home," says Ed. "It's a big part of why I do what I do today, so I can keep changing kid's lives, by just sending kids to camp."

Ed says that at age 17 he applied to work at Camp Tomahawk, but chose to join the Marine Corps instead, where he remained for six years before becoming a police officer for 27 years. However, he never broke ties with The Salvation Army or Camp Tomahawk, coming back to the Wheeling corps to volunteer and lead youth activities and helping out at the camp whenever possible.

"I'm always looking for ways to get back to Camp Tomahawk and help out wherever I can," he explains. "I'll go cut grass … I supervised the building of the camp's new fire circle and a few of the outdoor decks."

Retired Policeman

Upon retiring from the police department, Ed and his wife Goldie became Salvation Army officers, overseeing The Salvation Army youth and camp programs throughout the Maryland/West Virginia area. But Ed's camp experience came full circle as they now have four daughters, all of whom attended Camp Tomahawk. One of them is the camp's groundskeeper. Two grandchildren will both attend The Salvation Army's summer camps this summer.

Captains Ed and Goldie are also part of the team leading the Army's Baltimore Community Camp week in July, when 150 disadvantaged Baltimore area youth receive an activity filled, one–week residential camping experience at Camp Tomahawk at no expense to them or their families.

—Lafeea Watson submitted this article.

Captain Ed Long and his wife, Captain Goldie Long, are now corps officers in Weirton, WV.

Knowing God's Sufficiency
Miracle at a Mother/DaughterTea

"God still multiplies our gifts of love and service," says Major Donna Leedom, Women's Ministries Secretary. "Sophie Strickler has seen first-hand how His grace continues to show up in powerful ways. Sophie's gifts are those of help and service, especially catering. She loves preparing food and atmosphere as a gift of love for those she serves. Her offering has not gone unnoticed by the Lord. Here is her story."

Sophie Strickler

A College Freshman

"With only a few days left of my freshmen year of college, I was stressed as finals rapidly approached. I rushed home after a rigorous day of classes on campus to finish baking up delicious treats for our Mother/Daughter Tea that night at The Salvation Army Home League. With only a few hours left, and slowly running out of the essential ingredients, I finally finished my cooking.

"We had been planning for weeks all of the goodies we would prepare and serve at our tea. When I bake, everything has to be made from scratch. This added to my stress. After all my scones, mini cakes, and cream filled puff pastries were placed on the plates, I asked my mom how many we were expecting. She thought we would have at the most 24, which was exactly what I had prepared for.

"As the time came for the tea, the women began to arrive with their daughters, sisters, and mothers. It was wonderful to see so many familiar and new faces. However, I started to get nervous as the number of women quickly rose to more than 30. How were we going to feed all these women? I went to my mom with my concern and we thought of every way we could to make it work.

"'You and I just won't eat,' my mom said. I thought, well maybe I can break some of the scones in half, so we'll have more to go around.

"I went back into the kitchen and broke the scones down and brought enough plates down to the ladies for them to share with their tablemates. As I put the plates on each table, I discovered we had two extra plates. 'Well, that's odd,' I thought.

"The night was winding down; pictures were taken, devotions read and the food enjoyed. I looked around the room to see women wrapping up food to take home with them.

"'How can this be?' I asked myself. I had just enough food on each plate for the number of women at the tables. I was delighted that they all loved the food I had so carefully prepared, but I was most pleased that they had some to enjoy later.

> **Do you ever pray for God to demonstrate His power in your life?**

"After cleaning up the room, I went back to the kitchen with my mom and we were amazed at how much food was still left—half a box of mini cakes and even some scones! 'The Lord multiplied the food!' I told my mom. She looked at me in amazement and said, 'Yes, He did.'"

Sophie Strickler lives in Roseville, MN.

Putting People First
A Mentor and Volunteer

"But seek first his Kingdom and his righteousness, and all things will be given to you as well" (Matt. 6:33). This verse was given to me as a child when I was confirmed at the Lutheran church in Minneapolis. I gave my life to Christ that day, and my life took on greater meaning. I had a sense of appreciation and respect for the church and a desire to serve. Still, I did not fully realize the meaning of the verse until later in my life.

Lt. Mitcheal Brecto

After I graduated from college with a degree in accounting, I moved away from home and church to be closer to my job. I spent a period of time looking for the right church, but did not find one. I still had this burning desire to serve.

One day I heard that the Minneapolis Zoo was looking for volunteers and I quickly signed up. When I was not working at my regular job, you could find me at the zoo. The emptiness inside of me from not attending church was now being filled up with my service at the zoo.

After a few years, I found myself wanting to do even more, so I started volunteering for a Christian mentoring organization where they matched me up with a boy who did not have a father. Through the years I have mentored five boys.

Faith and Relationships

The family of one of the boys I mentored, Scotland, went to the local Salvation Army worship and community center. Every time his family invited me to church I would go. The experience I had at The Salvation Army was different from what I had known previously. Value was found in everyone. Also, a sense of community prevailed. The focus was not on ritual, but on providing for the needs of people through service and relationships. The church had discipleship, prayer groups, Bible studies and lots of fellowship. Faith was built on relationships.

With my experience of serving and mentoring, God had another plan for me, and that was to be a father. I had married Teresa and her four kids, Scotland being one of them. A year later we had a wonderful gift from God, our son Joshua.

Far Beyond Self

I was serving for the joy of serving, but still inside I was searching for more in my spirit. I soon became a Senior Soldier and kept busy at the corps by ringing bells, coordinating kettles, involvement in corps council and teaching Adventure Corps and Sunday school. I felt I had been given a special gift, and I wanted to share it with others.

In 2007, I was one of 11 people in Minnesota who received the "Eleven Who Care "award from the local TV station recognizing my outstanding volunteer efforts with The Salvation Army and Minneapolis Zoo. The inscription on the plaque reads, "like the caring tree that spreads its branches wide offering fruit for the hungry, shelter for the oppressed and beauty for the grieved, so gives the volunteer, branching far beyond the self into the family of life, meeting the needs of others with the selfless gift of love … born from the caring heart."

Since becoming a soldier, I put God's will and God's righteousness first in my life. Everything is now for Him. My family, my spouse, my volunteering, the work of my hands is for the Lord.

Lieutenant Mitcheal Brecto was ordained and commissioned as a Salvation Army officer on June 13, 2010 in Schaumburg, IL.

A Soldier In Two Armies
The Joy of Obedience

In 1983, I enlisted in the Oregon Army National Guard. I had been honorably discharged from the U.S. Navy in 1971. I was not living for God. I was: self–centered and a weekend drunk; addicted to cigarettes; embroiled in marriage problems; angry most of the time; read astrology books; believed in horoscopes; and liked to gossip.

Mathew Niblack

Discovering Joy

All that changed when I rededicated my life to Jesus Christ in 1984.

The Holy Spirit came into my body and began to dwell there. I was loved by God and I started loving myself. I learned to love my wife and children more. I started to learn how to love others, especially the downcast and the less fortunate.

I found out what real joy was. I learned how to laugh and have a good time without getting drunk. I began looking forward to getting up in the morning.

I started asking God for help. I knew that God was in control and that gave me real peace.

An Army Welcome

As a child, at the age of 5 or 6, I went to a Salvation Army Vacation Bible school in Wichita, Kansas. When I was 9 or 10, our family was stranded in Arizona and I remember eating a hot bowl of soup at a Salvation Army shelter. I had good memories of The Salvation Army and I knew in my heart that God led me to it.

I began attending a small Salvation Army church in Coos Bay, Oregon. Getting ready to go to my first service, a clear voice told me that I would not like going to church there and that it was filled with drug addicts and alcoholics. I knew where the voice came from and I renounced him and went to church anyway.

I felt I was "home" the first time I walked through the door. Captain Blix was a man who cared about people. When he preached, God's Word hit me in my heart and mind. I looked forward to going to church. After I went for a few Sundays, Mrs. Blix contacted my wife and soon she was attending with me. In fact, all three of our children started attending!

No More Addictions

On September 4, 1985, I was enrolled as a Salvation Army soldier. I asked God to take away my addictions to cigarettes and alcohol. I told Him that I could not serve Him in The Salvation Army with those addictions. He did! I no longer have any desire for alcohol or cigarettes.

God's Lead

I continued serving as a Salvation Army soldier after my National Guard term expired. Then my wife and I were asked to plant the Hillsboro, Oregon corps. We gladly accepted. We became auxiliary captains. In 1993 we were transferred to Newport, Oregon to start the corps there. My wife became very ill and we had to resign our commission. God opened a door for me and I accepted a job with the state employment division in Salem. I began attending The Salvation Army in Salem, became involved in street ministry and worked part–time at the Army's shelter as a case manager/job developer.

For God and Country

In January 2004, I inquired about returning to the National Guard. September 11, 2001 was always on my mind and I knew I had to do something for my country again. The recruiter told me I had to lose 60 pounds, pass the physical exam and get an age waiver approved (I was 55 years old at the time).

I asked God to remove the barriers if He wanted me to return to the military. He took away 60 pounds in six months, helped me pass the physical and got the age waiver approved in record time. People were amazed at what happened to me.

I am now serving in the National Guard part–time. I just returned from a 14–month deployment to Kuwait and I know God sent me there for a purpose. God has given me a ministry of singing the old gospel songs and witnessing for Him and continuing to help at the shelter.

Although I am a soldier of two armies, I like The Salvation Army best.

Mathew Niblack is a soldier at the corps in Salem, OR.

One Hot Day In Oklahoma
We Heard a Distant Drumbeat

My two siblings and I were living in two rooms above the Sand Springs, Oklahoma hardware store in 1934. I was 10. Our country was deep in the Great Depression. We were with our dad since mom's job was several miles away and she worked a minimum of 12 hours a day. Her employer would not allow any of us to stay with her.

Our playground was the roof of the adjoining building. We reached it by shinnying up and down the drain pipe.

Lena Holub and her family

As the eldest child, I was chief cook, bottle washer, baby sitter, and … you name it. Dad was out looking for work in the daytime and often played for dances in the evening, so we were often left to our own devices. One humid evening my sisters and I were at our playground trying to catch a stray breeze when I heard the beat of a drum in the distance. Believing it to be a parade, we proceeded to track it down.

It turned out to be a dozen people in a semi–circle in front of a bar. Some played instruments and others clapped their hands and fervently sang:

> *"Send the blessed tidings over vale and hill.*
> *'Tis the loving Savior calls the wanderer home.*
> *Whosoever will may come."*

Next a gentleman read some Bible passages. A few people stepped to the center of the group and told why they trusted Jesus as their Savior. There was more of that soul stirring band music. Then anyone who wanted could kneel by the big bass drum and ask Jesus to forgive them.

I had never heard about salvation. Now I learned that, even though I hadn't been a "good girl," God still loved me! I could ask for His forgiveness and He would give it to me!

I took my charges with me and we knelt down at that improvised altar. What joy I felt as I really gave my whole heart to Jesus!

I will always remember the nice lady who preached at this meeting. She prayed with me and made sure that I was serious about this step. I later learned her name was Captain Grace Thorne.

Marching To Church

After a time the group marched off to the accompaniment of the peppy music, some waving red, yellow, and blue flags, others rhythmically clapping and singing "Onward Christian Soldiers." We enthusiastically followed them into the church. We were made to feel welcome, so we stayed for our very first Salvation Service. We were also told about the children's programs.

Before long we were regulars, and loved it. We attended practically every time they opened the doors. We had found a home with people who cared about us. They treated us as family. We got lots of mothering from the women, especially the church–going ladies from the Widows Colony. Someone always came (usually with a real treat—fresh fruit) when one of us was ill.

At Christmas they not only gave us a big basket of food but also provided a fully–decorated Christmas tree, and new toys for each one of us! And, almost best of all, they allowed me to work at the officers' home (quarters in Army parlance) to earn money for a trip in a huge bus to attend a gigantic gathering for young people in Oklahoma City! I turned 11 that September and, in November of that year, I was proudly enrolled as a Junior Soldier.

Not long after, we moved from Sand Springs and lost touch

with the Army. We weren't able to connect with another corps until our mom had her sister moved us to Sheridan, Wyoming.

Oh, how I regret the time in between as I backslid several times. At long last, due to a severe injury, our Lord really got my attention. I'm now able to boldly say, "I will not, the Lord helping me, desert Him again!"

Today, 73 years later, I am still a "soldier bound for glory." The nearest corps is 130 miles away in Casper, Wyoming, but every time I am near a corps, I walk through the doors and feel I'm back home!

Many in my extended family are now Salvation Army soldiers and/or adherents, all because the Holy Spirit led a lost little girl to a distant drum.

Lena Holub lives in Thermopolis, WY.

2 Friendship Evangelism

"I no longer call you servants. Instead, I have called you friends, for everything that I learned from my Father I have made known to you."

John 15:14

God Answers Prayer
A Recovering Artist Shares Her Gift

Carol Kyle, retired Air Force widow, was looking for art supplies one Saturday morning when she saw a woman in full Salvation Army uniform. She immediately flashed back to her childhood when a Salvation Army captain had helped her family when they needed it.

Carol Kyle (left) with Sandra Hard

"Are you in The Salvation Army?" she asked Kathryn Barrett, who had just visited a nursing home in her capacity as Community Care Secretary in Panama City, Florida. Their conversation led Kathryn to invite Carol to the Home League, the women's ministry of The Salvation Army.

Soon Carol was attending Home League regularly and worshipping at the Salvation Army corps. Vibrant and interesting stories of her life around the world as an Air Force wife, pianist and painter became a part of the Home League programs in Panama City.

Unfortunately, Carol suffered a stroke two years ago, affecting the use of her right hand and impairing her speech and ability to walk. Undefeated, she strives to recover.

Playing the piano and painting had been part of her life for years. The loss of these creative outlets proved difficult for Carol. She prayed for God to move in this part of her recovery.

In speaking to her corps officer, Captain Marion Durham, she discovered that the captain's son, John–Luke, age 11, also had an affinity for art. She immediately offered her services as a private tutor for him to help him learn to draw and paint.

She hadn't picked up a paintbrush since her stroke, but she still had the desire, skill and passion to create. "If I can just encourage him and share with him what I've learned over the years, then it will be worth it," she told Captain Durham.

Little did she know that the Durhams had been praying for a way to afford art lessons for John–Luke, an expensive investment.

"The Lord had this planned all along. Carol needed a way to express herself through art again and we needed help in providing for John–Luke's creative endeavors," explains Captain Durham.

Carol remains undaunted in her efforts to recover. One day, when she was on one of her walks in her neighborhood with the aid of a cane, she saw Sandra Hard working in her yard a few houses down.

"I can't explain it," Sandra says, "I saw Carol and she looked like she needed a hug! So I went over to her and within minutes we realized we were both Christians and both painters."

Sandra had recently moved to the Panama City area and she was praying to find a women's Bible study. Carol invited her to the Home League.

Sandra and Carol now attend the women's group together. Carol gives Sandra advice on her artwork. Sandra checks on Carol and helps her as needed with physical concerns.

"I love it when we can see God's plans come together," says Captain Durham. "Sandra has become a wonderful member of the Women's Ministries, and Carol has a new friend right there on her street to check on her."

Carol now paints with her left hand and continues to work with John–Luke and Sandra on their art.

"I can't help but believe the Lord had this in mind all along," emphasizes the captain. "God answers prayer."

Carol Kyle lives in Panama City, FL.

Good Hunting
Finding a Common Language

I grew up in the U.S., and while I knew about The Salvation Army, I always thought of it as a Christian service agency more than as a church. In 2004, at the age of 24, I decided to move to Spain. I'd always wanted to live in another culture and speak Spanish, and I decided that there was no better time than the present. So I picked up and moved to Madrid, where I enrolled in a program to become an ESL teacher.

Lindsay and Estith Bonilla

My Spanish was shaky at best, so I was looking for an English–speaking church. One day Stacy, a Christian girl from my ESL program, invited me to go to a church she had heard about. Not relishing the idea of going church–hunting alone in an unfamiliar city, I gladly agreed. So the next Sunday morning I found myself in the Salvation Army's Madrid Central Corps.

Going It Alone

The service was entirely in Spanish, and I was amazed at how clearly I understood everything. At the end of the service, everyone came over to greet Stacy and me, and they invited us to the Youth Camp the following weekend. We made plans to attend; but at the last minute, Stacy called and said she wasn't going. I begged her—I couldn't go alone, I wouldn't be able to talk to anyone! But she refused, saying she had too much work to do. Now I was faced with a decision—go alone, knowing no one and speaking very little Spanish, or stay home, where I'd be safe but most likely bored too. I decided to go, and I'm so glad I did. While at times it was hard to communicate, it was at that camp that I began to develop relationships with people at the Madrid Corps.

God's Grace

God was gracious to me and helped bridge the language gap by giving me new friends in Jason, a soldier from England, and in Captain Gruer–Cauffield from Canada. The more time I spent with Jason and the captain, the more I got to know Estith, a soldier originally from Colombia. Estith and I were married a year and–a–half ago in my hometown of Akron, Ohio, where we are now part of the Akron Citadel Corps. We were very fortunate to share our wedding day with both Jason (best man) and Captain Gruer–Cauffield (officiate) who came all the way from Madrid to celebrate with us. I truly believe the Holy Spirit was at work in every detail—from Stacy's invitation, to understanding the sermon that day, to giving me the courage to go to the camp alone, to bringing Estith and I together—and I am grateful to the Lord for guiding me to The Salvation Army where I have so many opportunities to live out my belief that we are "Saved to Serve."

> **I truly believe the Holy Spirit was at work in every detail.**

Lindsay Bonilla is a soldier at the corps in Akron, OH .

I Got A Bargain
Army Programs Sealed the Deal

A few years ago I stepped into the Bargain Center on Third Ave. in Marshalltown, Iowa. The building used to be the home of The Salvation Army before it moved to State Street in 1975.

I stood where I had knelt in 1974 to accept Jesus Christ as my Lord and Savior. Before that day I was religious but lost. I attended church but was empty and searching inside. A friend at school invited me to volleyball night sponsored by The Salvation Army. We met at Riverview Park

Ken Locke

during the summer, playing volleyball, sharing snacks (a real draw for a teenager in high school) and praying before leaving. They welcomed me with open arms. I didn't know anything about The Salvation Army, and was surprised when they invited me to their weekly Bible study. I attended and was amazed how openly they studied the Word together with their woman pastor, Major Rema Fellman. I had to learn more about these strangely attired people!

Testimony Time

One Sunday night I joined them for their evening Salvation Meeting. Folks popped up during the testimony time and shared their relationship with Jesus. He was not a concept, but a real person to them! Some of them came in before the meeting talking about how they had just been to the "open air." I asked Major Rema after the meeting if I could join them next week for their open air service. She smiled and told me what time they left.

Next Sunday I came to the Army and we prayed before getting into the station wagons. We pulled up and parked at the Courthouse on Main Street as these uniformed crazies grabbed their instruments and drum, forming a circle. The major had a loudspeaker in hand. I wanted to dig a hole and hide when I saw some guys down the street that would make school fun on Monday! After some music and singing these Salvationists started giving their testimonies right there in the center of town. I was praying for the open air to end when the major introduced me and asked if I wanted to share. I mumbled a few religious thoughts and jumped back into the circle.

> **The emptiness I felt and the ache in my heart grew.**

An Emptiness

The emptiness I felt and the ache in my heart grew as we rode back to the corps. That evening the major shared about being born again, about forgiveness of sins and a personal relationship with Christ. During the altar call they sang, "Turn Your Eyes Upon Jesus" as I knelt, wanting what they had. That night I received more than a bargain, I received the gift of salvation and a relationship with the Son of God, Jesus Christ.

The place where I knelt is now gone. Many of those who shared their testimonies and love with me 30 years ago have been "promoted to glory," seeing the Savior face to face. But Christ is faithful. He is the same yesterday, today and forever! When I met this strange Army, I received salvation through Jesus Christ! To God Be the Glory!

Ken Locke serves as the community ministries director for The Salvation Army in Warsaw, IN.

New Life in Community
Manna for a Volunteer's Soul

I seemed to have my head on straight, but it was all a lie which ended a year ago when my employer realized I had embezzled a large sum of money. Heading to jail for six months, I knew I had ruined my life. With my husband and kids waiting for me on the outside, I was all alone and depressed in my jail cell with no end in sight.

It all changed when I was given the opportunity to do community service. Instead of staying in my cell 24/7 I got to go out five days

Kendra Mahar, Brenda Bricker, and Maryann Slaght.

a week to our local Salvation Army. I only knew of The Salvation Army for their holiday bell ringing fundraisers. I had no idea what they really stood for.

Forgive Myself?

The gift of The Salvation Army started with a friendly smile and understanding from Barb, who helped me get through my first morning in the kitchen while I suffered through an anxiety attack. Then every day for over five months, as I organized donations for resale or prepared and served meals in the soup kitchen, a new world slowly opened up to me.

My counselor emphasized how it was so important to forgive myself and not until then would I be able to build a better life for myself and my family. I knew I had humiliated my family and had broken several of God's commandments. I just couldn't see how I could forgive myself for what I had done and move on with my life. I ached terribly for the sins I had committed.

It wasn't long before I learned that it took a lot of people to make The Salvation Army run. Then one day I realized that this was more than a fundraising organization. It was a Church of God and their ministry touched everyone in the community. The volunteers and employees of the corps were missionaries and soon I was one of their followers.

Acceptance

Not once throughout this terrible ordeal did I feel judged inside The Salvation Army—from Captain Scott giving me a smile and Wanda and Brenda giving me hugs to John and Chris giving me a friendly ear. They all opened their arms and accepted me as one of their own.

I made a lot of friends, too many to mention, and soon I could see myself turning into someone I could be proud of.

I've completed my sentence, but not my association with The Salvation Army. I want to be a missionary for God at the corps. I still volunteer at the store and attend church on Sundays and Bible study on Tuesday. I feel God's love and I am slowly gaining the confidence to forgive myself and make a better life for my family.

Kendra Mahar lives in Kincheloe, MI.

Influence Is Leadership
Passing the Torch

I am a first generation
Salvationist, but my path to
officership runs deep. I was
introduced to The Salvation Army,
to my salvation, and to my calling
by three generations of Salvationists from one family— my friend,
her mother, and her grandmother.

Three Generations
When I was in the fifth grade the
youngest of the three generations
was in my grade at school. One
day she invited me to come to
church with her at The Salvation

Captain Fallyn Garrison

Army where her parents were the corps officers.

The more I attended the corps, the more I loved being there.
Her mother was my favorite teacher. She taught me about God
and about His Son. She taught me about the need for salvation.
Through the ministry of these two generations I eventually
accepted Christ as my Savior when I attended Youth Councils
when I was a teenager.

Years later, after I was married, I was introduced to the third
generation of this Salvationist family. My husband and I had
started attending The Salvation Army where my childhood
friend's grandmother also attended. When she was diagnosed
with cancer we would go to her home and visit her. It was during
our last visit that God used her to call us into officership.

In the book of Joshua, after Moses passes away, God passes
the leadership torch from one generation to the next. God says to

Joshua (the next generation), "Do not let this Book of the Law depart from your mouth; meditate on it day and night, so that you may be careful to do everything written in it. Then you will be prosperous and successful. Have I not commanded you? Be strong and courageous. Do not be terrified; do not be discouraged, for the Lord your God will be with you wherever you go" (Joshua 1:8-9).

In my life, God used three generations of Salvationists to prepare me for officership by teaching me the Scriptures and their message. Now he is passing the torch to me. I am confident of the task set before me because I know God will be right by my side the whole time. He will use the knowledge I gained from these three generations to influence many generations to come.

Captains Fallyn and Nicholas Garrison were appointed as corps officers in Louisville, KY in June 2006.

Good Samaritans
Small Kindness Sows Priceless Blessings

We are first generation Salvationists. My husband and I had just come out of a local restaurant when a couple of ladies asked us about our car. Its license plates indicate that my husband is a veteran.

When my husband informed the ladies of this, they told us they were from The Salvation Army. They had a basket of items to be given to veterans and asked if we

Tyler, Jim and Esther Eley

knew any veterans we could give them to. We told them we would be happy to deliver them and they told us to come the next day to pick the basket up.

Tyler Liked It

When we arrived they were having church services. When we started to leave, a gentleman told us that it was alright to come in anyway. After the first song our son, who is autistic, said "I like this church. Can we come back?"

We had been looking for somewhere to go where we would feel comfortable and not condemned for our son's disability. And he was very comfortable at the Army.

Ministry Opportunities

Almost three years later I am the Community Care Ministries

Secretary, and a Women Ministries member. My husband is the Junior Soldier Sergeant as well as the corp representatives for Veterans. Our son is a Junior Soldier as well as an usher and helps run the overhead projector.

We thank the Lord for bringing us together and giving us the peace we had been seeking for so long, and for giving us such good friends and extended family.

Esther, Jim and Tyler Eley are soldiers in the corps in Eugene, OR .

No Condemnation
Finding Faith Through Friends

Major Connie DeMichael and I have been blessed by the spiritual growth of the women in the Women's Ministries Bible studies here in Wilmington, Delaware held at her home on Tuesday evenings. We have witnessed conversions, growth in holiness and commitments to soldiership and local officer positions.

One source of blessing for us has been Betty Anunziata. Betty was raised Catholic and as a young girl lived in both a deten-tion center and a Catholic home

Betty Anunziata

for girls in upstate New York. She was married more than once and drifted from faith. In her retirement years, she was brought to Women's Ministries by Joyce Liott, one of our soldiers. Joyce is a bubbly, vibrant young Christian woman. The Spirit radiates in her face and her love for others spills over into the lives of those around her every day. She has been overjoyed to lead people to Christ, and to help other Christians along the way to heaven.

Prayer Support

Her prayerful support and friendship aided Betty's spiritual journey. Betty eagerly dug into the Bible for the first time in her life. Each week, as she discovered new truths about her Savior, she would enthusiastically declare, "I wish I had known this fifty years ago!"

The Holy Spirit led her to the corps on Sundays and then to

soldiership. Currently she is an active participant in Discipleship Training, beginning Level II.

Betty says, "At the time I became a Salvationist I was a Catholic who did not attend church—had not—for a very long time. During that time I missed God and always felt a little guilty, but managed to overrule my guilt with my own rationalizations. Then I met Joyce, a Salvationist, and she invited me to the Salvation Army church and ladies Bible study. I never really felt close to God because of my lifestyle at that time. But I immediately felt a part of the Army. I began to feel closer to God than ever before.

"I know I am a sinner. But it doesn't bog me down. God loves me, in spite of my sin! It is a message of love, not condemnation. I feel love and compassion from God I never felt before. I am truly glad I am a Salvationist."

—Major Ruth Bartholomew, who wrote this article, is a corps officer in Wilmington, DE.

Betty Anunziata is a soldier in the Salvation Army corps in Wilmington, DE.

Good Friends
Intimacy at a Philadelphia Corps

We moved onto Ontario Street in Philadelphia when I was four years old. I don't really remember much about my early days on the block, but at some point my mom met Carol Daly, who lived across the street from us.

Mary Parks and her friend Lizz Murray

After building a friendship with my mom, grandmom and me, Carol eventually invited me to Sunbeams at The Salvation Army Philadelphia Pioneer corps. Through my involvement with the Sunbeam program, I began to get involved in other corps programs, like Sunday School and the Holiness Meeting. Each week, Carol and her family invited me to walk or ride with them to the corps.

Music

As I made friends, I became more interested in other activities, such as music and arts school and the Junior Soldier program. I eventually went on to become a corps cadet, band member and songster. As I progressed musically, I was privileged to participate in an award winning Junior Songster brigade, the PenDel Youth Band and Chorus and eventually the PenDel Brass and Singers, where I was the first female tuba player in that illustrious group.

I continued to be active in the corps and developed friendships to the point where I considered the corps my second home. These bonds would prove vital when, in 2000, my mom suffered a massive stroke which ultimately took her life ten days before my 21st birthday. Although they both had plans for that day, Priscilla and Bernice, two women from the corps whom I consider to be adoptive "moms," walked me through the difficult tasks of preparing for my mom's final arrangements. They took me to the hospital when the doctor called to inform me of my mom's passing, and stayed with me to support me when I was all alone.

After my mom's passing, I fell into a deep depression. As a result, I lost the apartment which I had lived in with my mom and grandmom. When others would have had me go into the city's shelter system, Sandy, another "mom," took me under her wing and allowed me to stay with her for a season. She not only gave me a place to stay, but a place that I could call "home." There are many others who have played an essential role in my spiritual growth. This family bond reached beyond adoptive "moms" to "brothers" and "sisters" as well.

Surprise

When my 25th birthday rolled around, a group of dear friends from the corps got together and managed to throw me a surprise party. This seemingly small gesture meant the world to me and served as a reminder that I have people who care about me, even when it seems as if no one does.

I am currently in college studying multimedia development, and hope to use these skills in my personal ministry. I developed and ran multimedia for both the Pioneer and the GeneratioNext corps. Recently I also had the opportunity to design and run computer presentations at our divisional Soldier's Rally and Youth Councils and have also been asked to assist in setting up presentations for another corps in our division. In my heart, this is a present–day means of adapting our measures to the times in which we live.

Mary Parks is a soldier at the Philadelphia Pioneer corps.

3 Family Evangelism

"My mother and brothers are those who hear
God's Word and put it into practice."

Luke 8:21

Morganton Memories
"Let's Give The Salvation Army a Try"

In 1999, I found myself without a church home after being a member of a congregation for many years. My husband, who was not attending church at the time, kept asking me why we didn't try The Salvation Army. The Army had opened a church in our area just a year or two before this.

My husband had good memories of the Army because his grandmother had belonged when he was a child and had proudly worn the uniform and worked the kettles at Christmas

Penny Helton

time. Also he had fond memories of how The Salvation Army helped the military personnel when he was in the U.S. Army in Korea.

Welcomed Home

I had kidney cancer and the first Sunday that I was able to be in church after my surgery found us at the Morganton, North Carolina Salvation Army corps. We never visited any other church after that. I felt at home and welcomed by Captains David and Shirley Chapman and the small congregation. Eventually we were joined by our son, Danny, and his family which included his wife and two small sons. We have many happy memories of the corps and our involvement there. My husband also attended regularly as long as our corps stayed open.

It was a very active corps even though it was small. We had an after school program, vacation Bible school every summer, visitation to prisons and nursing homes and other outreach. In 2000, I became a soldier and was the adult Sunday school teacher. Our women's group was active, although I didn't always get to attend due to my work schedule as a hospice nurse. I loved taking a week off in December to help Captain Shirley with the Christmas outreach.

I was able to attend many meetings in Atlanta, women's camps and other seminars. The most memorable of these was the International Congress in 2000.

Also, in 2000 I went to England to a penpal conference. A friend of a penpal took the train from Welling to London and met me and took me to the Salvation Army Regent Hall there in London. She had heard about me and my involvement with the Army through my penpal in Wales, and wanted to meet me, since she also belonged to The Salvation Army and was still very active in the corps in Welling, Kent. She has become a good friend, and although she is not a regular penpaller like I am we correspond regularly and I hope to visit her again someday.

Captains David and Shirley Chapman recently performed the funeral of our son, who died unexpectedly. Our daughter–in–law requested that they be involved in the service in this way and they gladly accepted, even though this was very difficult for them.

Our little corps had to close ...

Unfortunately, our little corps had to close a few years ago. I have not given up hope that someday it will be able to reopen. I still remain involved in the Army by subscribing to the *War Cry* and being involved in the Soup and Supper program in the community and in the International Children's Sponsorship program.

Penny Helton lives in Morganton, NC.

No Bonnet for Me!
Doing Things the Hard Way

I didn't grow up in The Salvation Army, but I had four aunts who were members. I didn't believe in women preachers and surely did not want to wear the same thing each Sunday. After all, women needed to dress properly, and "grandma shoes" did not fit into my lifestyle. The bonnet was too old–fashioned. Soon I would have to eat those words, and they were hard to swallow.

Anna Vetterl Wilkerson

Lessons from God

In 1960, I became a Salvationist for economic reasons. I was living with one of my Salvationist aunts on one side of town. My church was on the other side and neither of us drove, so we went to her church. It was closer and we could share the taxi fare.

I hadn't attended too long when the captain asked me to teach a Sunday school class. So for two years, I taught the primary class at the Salvation Army corps in Anniston, Alabama. I loved teaching those children. I didn't realize that as I was teaching them, God was teaching me.

The Right Way

My soon–to–be husband was there in Anniston all the time, attending the same corps. We started dating and fell in love. When we married, we left for Biloxi, Mississippi to begin our lives together and to get on–the–job training. One of our first jobs was to sell the

War Cry. So I prepared to don the bonnet and the uniform. (I never did wear "grandma shoes," but today I come close.)

First of all, I could not tie the sash on the bonnet and told my husband, "No, I won't wear it." He said that I should wear it completely and proudly or not at all. Well, the more I thought about it, the more I came to the conclusion that if I was going to do this, I'd better do it properly. After several attempts, I finally formed some reasonable bow on the ribbon. I was unaware that I could have had it tied one time and just used a snap to put it in place. Then again, I have never been known to do things the easy way.

Anna in her bonnet in 1958. Her husband encouraged her to wear it completely.

He Knows Best

With the bonnet intact, I was off to sell the *War Cry.* I prayed, "Dear Lord, please let the first person I ask buy a *War Cry* and then I can keep on going."

Do you think He answered my prayer? Yes, but not in the way I wanted. I believe that first person said no so I would not give up.

I'm sorry that the bonnet is no longer worn in our area. In other parts of the world it's still a part of a "lassie's" attire. Will it ever come back? I don't know, but it will always be a part of my life—it will remind me of the time I had to learn humility.

I am so happy to declare "I'm a first generation Salvationist." My two children and four grandchildren also faithfully attend our corps in Huntsville, Alabama.

Anna Vetterl Wilkerson is a Salvation Army soldier in Huntsville, AL.

Turning Points
Prayer and the Word

I am the oldest of four brothers. When I was 11 years old my mom and dad separated and that is when we started attending church.

I came to know about God's saving grace while in a Sunday school class. From that time on, we were very faithful in going to church. At the age of 15 my parents got back together, but in our home the best example of being a Christian was lived out by my mom.

Lt. Joseph Cisneros

A Leader

My mother was the spiritual leader in our home. She saw to it that we went to church. Looking back, I see that this was an important turning point in my life.

After joining the Air Force at 19, I started to share my faith, but I was not attending church. So I was starting to lose some of the teachings that are fundamental to a Christian walk. My second turning point came when I was sent to England. I decided that what I was doing was neither satisfying nor fulfilling. I began attending church services again. I started to read the word of God intensely and finally moved into a Christian men's home for singles, where I was engulfed in God's Word and in prayer.

My Desire

I felt the need to go out and speak God's Word to everyone. I knocked on doors, led street evangelism and even preached in open–air services.

I spent nine years praying for my future wife, even though I had not met her yet. After six years in England I was moved to Phoenix where I met my wife Dina. We both felt a call to preach and teach. We prayed for over a year about where God would want to use us in full–time ministry.

Joseph and Dina Cisneros

Our Calling

We met The Salvation Army through my brother–in–law in August 2001. We went for an interview and Major Syolor asked us many questions about our calling. One month after the tragic events of 9/11, we moved to Oregon to take over the work in the Woodburn Temple Corps. We did what was asked of us and many came to the Lord. God reaffirmed His calling in our lives. We felt God wanted us to be Salvation Army officers.

Many people have prayed and worked with us to get us where we are today. We have enjoyed our time at the College for Officer Training at Crestmont, and now we are more prepared to enter the ranks of those fighting for lost souls. Wherever the Lord calls us we are ready to go. To God be the Glory!

Lieutenant Joseph Cisneros was ordained and commissioned as a Salvation Army officer on June 14, 2009 in Cerritos, CA.

God Has Been So Good
The Ripple Effect Of One Invitation

"God has been so good to me and my family, I just want everyone to know!" exclaims Lluvia Urguia who, along with her husband, Hugo, attends the Long Beach, CA Corps. This sentiment toward God is a far cry from her life just three years ago when her family was in shambles. Lluvia and her father, Angel Rodriguez, had a very destructive relationship. Her mother, Angelica, was desperate for help.

Lluvia and Hugo Urguia

Through a connection Angelica had with someone attending the Latino Ministry of the Long Beach Home League, she accepted an invitation and began attending. Angelica began to bring her younger daughter Vanessa, and her baby, Alex to The Salvation Army. Lluvia and her father continued their constant arguing until Angel began to notice a change in his wife.

Peace and Calm

"I noticed she was so calm, she had peace, even when we didn't. I wanted to know how she could be this way," Angel shared. Soon he began attending the Sunday Spanish service and the Men's Fellowship.

Lluvia admits she was skeptical about the changes she began to see in both her parents. "I really didn't know what to think. They were changing, and I wasn't sure it was serious." But she knew it was a reality when her father came to her and apologized for his behavior and vowed to show her he was different because he now had a relationship with Jesus Christ. That's when Lluvia decided she had to experience this for herself.

Lluvia and her then fiancé, Hugo, began attending The Salvation Army and soon felt the need to develop a relationship with Jesus Christ. Shortly after getting married, both she and Hugo, along with her parents and her younger sister, became Senior Soldiers of the Long Beach Corps.

"She had peace, even when we didn't."

Today Lluvia and Hugo are active members and they plan to enter training school to become Salvation Army officers.

"All this came to my family through the invitation of one faithful woman who invited my mom to Home League at The Salvation Army, so I am always inviting others to church!" she says. "You never know how much God can use you to help bring a God–sized change to someone's life."

—*Captain Kory Acosta, the writer, is a corps officer at the Corps Community Center in Santa Fe Springs, CA.*

Lluvia and Hugo Urguia are from Long Beach, CA.

Beyond Disappointment
Doing Great Things for God and the Army

Michelle had to endure moving quite a bit as a young child. Born to Linda and Le'Noel Bond on a ranch just outside of Duran, Oklahoma, she ended up attending 11 schools in 12 years.

Michelle attended many Baptist churches when she was growing up. At a young age she came to know Jesus as her Savior. Later, at the age of 23, Michelle went

Captain Laura Pedraza with Michelle Copelin

to a Christian camp where she met wonderful people who not only loved Jesus, but had an understanding of the Holy Spirit. They helped Michelle let go of the hurts and disappointments of her teenage years and told her that God had a plan for her life.

Bill and Ben

A few years later she met her future husband Bill Copelin and, after three years, they were blessed with their son Ben. Michelle was able to give up her job as a school teacher and stay at home with her son with Bill working as a vice–president for J.B. Hunt, Inc. As Ben grew into his teenage years, Michelle started volunteer work with a ministry in Fayetteville, Arkansas called Life Source.

She was later introduced to The Salvation Army by her husband. He told her, "Michelle, I have met some wonderful Christian people." Michelle, who didn't know much about The Salvation Army, was intrigued by her husband's enthusiasm and had agreed to meet with the new people. After meeting with them, she knew that God was starting a new chapter in her life.

After that meeting Michelle and her family started attending the Salvation Army Springdale, Arkansas Corps where Captains Alejandro and Laura Pedraza are in command. She was greeted with a great welcome from the corps family. After some time attending she made the commitment to be enrolled as an Adherent. She and Bill were enrolled on April 23, 2006, she as an Adherent, he as a Senior Soldier.

Michelle grew more and more involved with volunteer work and accepted an invitation from her corps officers to be the Angel Tree coordinator for the Springdale Corps.

She has done great things for God and for the Army, such as:

• Finding a warehouse for Angel Tree
• Coordinating Volunteers
• Spending hours and hours at the warehouse
• Getting involved with Women's Ministry
• Taking a leadership role as Sunday School teacher
• Putting time and effort into a Mexico project
• Taking charge of the decor of the corps building.
• Hosting the corps council meeting

"Michelle and Bill have helped us achieve a lot of our goals because of the wonderful influence they have with the people in the Springdale community," says Captain Laura Pedraza.

The Copelins also had the opportunity to travel to Israel and continue to pray for that country. They brought a flag back from Israel which they gave to the corps as a reminder to pray constantly for Jerusalem.

—Captain Laura Pedraza wrote this article.

Michele and Bill Copelin live in Springdale, AR.

Gifts of a Corps Volunteer
Prayer Warrior, Teacher and Treasurer

Corps Sergeant Major Maggie McNitt is the heart, soul, hands and feet of the North Central Brevard, Florida corps. She may be small in stature but she is great in spirit and service.

Sergeant Major Maggie McNitt

She was born in Worcester, Massachusetts and raised in the Baptist church, where she attended tent meetings. Her mother was an evangelical Christian. Maggie graduated as a registered nurse from Henry Ford Hospital in Detroit, Michigan in 1950. She served for 50 years as a nurse and retired in 1998.

A Prayer Warrior

She is a prayer warrior who says prayer got her through nurses' training and her career.

She has two daughters who live in Arizona and Florida, and one son who is director of Mission International. He and his family do missionary work in the Middle East and Africa. He recently returned from a visit to an underground church in Cairo, Egypt.

Her Husband Was A Member

Maggie met The Salvation Army through her husband, Mickey, who was an adherent of the Titusville, Florida corps. She became a soldier in 1982 and corps sergeant major in 1986. Maggie loves the Lord and is willing to do anything the Army needs her to do. She is now teaching the Junior Soldier class. She is treasurer of the Home League and makes it her responsibility to gather items and sort and price them for our annual yard sale. She also gets other soldiers and volunteers to help in the sale.

She Helps At Christmas

> **Corps Sergeant Major Maggie McNitt is the heart, soul, hands and feet of the North Central Brevard corps.**

For the past three years, she has been responsible for distributing toys and canned foods at Christmas. She and her helpers spend many hours sorting canned goods, packing bags, securing toys and making the bags for each child. She gets volunteers to help her with the distribution.

May God continually bless Maggie McNitt for her faithfulness to the Lord and The Salvation Army. She is a true example of the spirit of the Army and the spirit of Jesus, her Savior.

—Major Sharon E. Owens wrote this article.

Maggie McNitt volunteers for the North Central Brevard, FL corps.

Dying A Slow Death
God Threw Us a Lifeline

I was born in Puerto Rico, the second of five sisters. I was raised in a Christian home because my father was the pastor of a Pentecostal church. Since we were the pastor's daughters, people thought we needed to be "perfect." I remember how strict my parents were with us all the time. I always wanted to live in such a way that my parents wouldn't hear complaints about me. I used to go to church because my parents wanted me to go, and because I thought that just by attending church I would be safe.

Lt. Zaida Rivera

At the age of 10, I accepted Christ as my Savior, and from then on I've served Him. My sister in law, Gloryvee, had at one time attended The Salvation Army. I remember her telling me about this new church that she had found and about all the fun things they did with the Women's Ministry, Sunbeams and other corps programs.

In 2004, there was a Christmas Spectacular at the Army corps she attended. She invited me and my family to go to the meeting, and even though I hesitated at first, I decided to go. The minute I stepped into the building, I felt mixed emotions. By the end of the night, I was ready to go home, but my husband and kids were so excited because they had attended the programs and they were ready to stay at the Army.

I remember my husband and kids saying that we should attend the Army. I told them not to even say that as a joke. They thought I was being funny, so we left it like that. What I didn't know was that God had something different planned for us.

"I'm Dying Spiritually"

In the next few months, everything seemed to go wrong. We started to have difficulties at home and also at the church we were attending. I remember it got so bad that one day my husband came home from work and said to me, "If we don't move to another church, I might as well stay home, because I'm dying spiritually." What I didn't know was that this conversation would change the rest of our lives. I asked my husband, "What do you want to do?"

"Well, let's go visit The Salvation Army," he replied.

The following Sunday we went to the corps, and when the officer finished his sermon, he said, "God is telling me that there's someone in this place who is arguing about whether they should move or not." Of course, I told myself, "He's not talking to me," but he was! During the invitation after the sermon, I went to the altar. The officer and corps members prayed for me and my entire family, and from that point on, we have been part of The Salvation Army.

God's Guidance

Because both my husband and I had a calling to ministry when we were young, we decided to pray for the Lord's guidance. God opened the door for us to go to the School for Officer Training. If I tell you that life has been easy, I would be lying; but I can tell you that God has made a way where I didn't see a way.

"I waited patiently for the Lord; he turned to me and heard my cry. He lifted me out of the slimy pit, out of the mud and mire; he set my feet on a rock and gave me a firm place to stand" (Psalm 40:1–2).

Lieutenant Zaida Rivera was ordained and commissioned as a Salvation Army officer on June 14, 2009 in White Plains, NY.

No More Excuses
Becoming Intentional

When I was a child I attended Methodist and Baptist churches. When I became an adult my aunt would tell me stories of her new church and how she wanted me to come and visit. I always found excuses for not going until she asked me if my son could attend youth activities at the Salvation Army corps.

Lt. Kellie Cantrell

The atmosphere there made such a positive influence on my son that he asked me to come see the program he was involved in.

The day I walked into the corps in Cartersville, Georgia, I felt God's love and acceptance, but I wasn't ready to listen to the message that God was sending me through The Salvation Army.

Not Enough

My day–to–day life was leaving me in constant misery. The emptiness in my heart confirmed that God had plans for me. I thought that immersing myself in the corps and its programs would be enough for God—and enough for my heart to be filled. But the emptiness was still there. Teaching Sunday school and being the Young People's Sergeant–Major did not satisfy my desire to be more, to draw closer to God. There were days of constant crying, praying and questioning before God.

One day my corps officers, Captains Doug and Storm McClure, asked to have a conversation with me, and told me they had a message from God for me. It was so simple, yet so extraordinary. The message was "You would make a great officer."

Immediately I thought "No way, that is not the life for me." I started running from my calling. I proceeded to make some wrong choices, and ended up turning to material things for comfort.

Then one day our CSM, Hazel Lord, came to me with

an opportunity to preach. She advised me to go home, pray, and let her know my answer. My prayers that night consisted of asking God to give me excuses, so the obligation of speaking His Word would not fall upon me.

Instead of getting the answers I wanted, God provided me with a sermon and told me that it was my obligation and I needed to obey His calling for my life.

On a cold October morning, as I prepared to walk up to the pulpit to deliver God's message, I found myself surrounded by the Holy Spirit. As the words flowed from my mouth, I submitted to letting God be in control.

What God Wanted

The people's response to God's message that day was amazing! I knew exactly what God wanted me to do, but still I came up with excuses. I told myself that I was comfortable with my life as it was, and that I did not need to become a Salvation Army officer in order to reach people.

At the corps we started the Bible study, "If you want to walk on water, you have got to get out of the boat." God showed me that I made excuses so I could stay in my comfort zone. He showed me that I needed to go where the need was greatest and that He was the one to decide just when and where that was. I knew then that I would become an officer, and would leave myself behind, and that I would have 100% percent faith in God.

> **The emptiness in my heart confirmed that God had plans for me.**

Listening to God's instructions is not always easy, but following His path for my life is indescribable. Knowing that God is always in control brought the peace and understanding that had been missing from my life and heart. I now strive to submit to God and follow Him.

Lieutenant Kellie Cantrell was ordained and commissioned as a Salvation Army officer on June 6, 2010 in Atlanta, GA.

4 All the World

"And I will shake all nations, and what is desired by all nations will come: and I will fill this house with glory, says the Lord Almighty."

Haggai 2:7

Peter's Words Moved Me
A Life of Sacrificial Service

After I graduated from a university, I worked as a tutor for children and teenagers. I met my husband at my work place. He had already decided to be a Salvation Army officer. Unlike other Christians, he didn't push me to accept Jesus Christ as a Savior. He just gave me the Bible. I had never had a Bible before and was very curious. A few months later, I went to his Salvation Army corps with him.

Captain Junghee Hwang

Even though my parents didn't want me to go to church, I kept going and kept reading the Bible and other Christian books. At the beginning, I couldn't believe and accept what the Bible said. I had many questions and doubts in my mind. I could call God "God," but I couldn't call Him "Lord" or "Father."

Unsure How to Pray

I didn't think I knew how to pray to God, but I prayed, "God, if you really exist, let me see you. Talk to me. Make me understand and believe Your words."

One day I was reading the words of Peter's confession: Jesus asked Peter, "Who do you say I am?" Peter confessed, "You are the Christ, the Son of the living God!" Suddenly tears poured out of my eyes. I just couldn't stop crying. I felt so sorry to God and I confessed, "Lord, you are my Father." After that, God helped me believe everything in the Bible.

Later, my husband and I went to New Zealand to help in a Korean corps there. I served as a Sunday School teacher. I did my best and I was loved by the people in the corps. God gave me a great opportunity to go to the Discipleship Training School in Canada. I also went to Guatemala on a mission trip, serving in many churches there for two months.

During that time, I had to sacrifice a lot. I had to share everything I had— food, money, room and time. I really felt that living this way

The Hwang family

was the way Christians should live. It was such a time of blessing. I started every single day with worship and prayer. Whenever I went out for street evangelism, I felt the Holy Spirit was working through me. God made me realize how much and how eagerly He wanted to use me.

This was when He gave me the scripture that confirmed my calling to be a Salvation Army officer: "Before I formed you in the womb I knew you, before you were born I set you apart; I appointed you as a prophet to the nations" (Jer. 1:5).

God was with me when I denied Him. God was with me when I doubted Him. And God is with me right now.

Captain Junghee Hwang was ordained and commissioned as a Salvation Army officer on June 11, 2007 in the EasternTerritory.

Fisher of Men
Energized by My Family's Faith

I was born in a Christian home, and as I was growing up I always had an unwavering belief in the Christian life, its ethics and morals.

When my family and I came to the United States from El Salvador, we started to look for a church to attend. It was not more than a week before my mother found the Salvation Army Hollywood corps. My mother's passion and devotion to God and our attendance at the corps put me in contact with all the Army's activities and youth programs.

Captain Rene Carcamo

Rededication

At age 17, I rededicated my life to Christ during a prayer meeting at the corps. I also met my wife during a youth program; we had a seven year "on and off" relationship.

During those seven years, my wife completed training and was commissioned as an officer. When our relationship resumed, we got married, which required my wife to step out of officership. We lived in Denver for the next nine years and were active in the local corps.

> **I am dedicating my life to Him more and more. I am willing to be His faithful and obedient servant.**

My wife prayed constantly to return to officership and for me to receive the same calling to serve the Lord, not only as His disciple but also as a "fisher of men."

Her fervent prayers were answered and I too felt a longing to serve God in a more meaningful manner. God placed His call into my heart for officership. I was obedient to His call and I am now ready, faithful and willing to do His ministry wherever He sends me to preach His Word.

The Carcamo family

In return for God's faith and unwavering love for me, I am dedicating my life to Him. I am willing to be His faithful and obedient servant.

Passion for Hispanic Ministry

In my journey with the Lord, I will respond to His call and lay down my life in service to those who hunger for and seek the Word of our Lord. I have a passion for Hispanic ministry, for youth and children. And I have a desire to help people in need.

Captain Rene Carcamo was ordained and commissioned as a Salvation Army officer on June 11, 2006 in the Western Territory.

Shaken By An Earthquake
I Learned to Stand on Solid Rock

I wasn't "in trouble." I was a good kid. I felt that I was all "grown–up" and it was just time for me to "leave the nest," so my mother let me go.

On September 19, 1985, the foundation of my world was rocked. By that time I was living in picturesque Mexico City, Mexico. A beautiful, tranquil morning became ugly and violent. An earthquake, the worst in Mexican history, shook the city.

I lived on the fifth floor of an apartment building. Instantly,

Captain Gabriela Rangel

my world was transformed. Chaos and confusion were very real. I was afraid.

Somehow I managed to get down the staircase. Once outside, the noise of sirens was deafening. Smoke darkened the sky. The smell of death filled the air. I wanted the nightmare to end. I wanted my mother.

For several days I tried to communicate with her to tell her that I was alright, that I was safe, that I was alive. My attempts proved futile. I grew frustrated and discouraged. Hopelessness held me captive.

It was in this state of loneliness and self–pity that I first met The Salvation Army. A man wearing a strange looking military uniform had been looking specifically for me. He had been deployed to Mexico City to assist in the disaster relief work. He had a letter from my mom inviting me to come home. This man was my mom's pastor. My mother had begun to attend church services at The Salvation Army.

I returned to my childhood home. On occasion, I would attend church activities with my mom. This made her very happy. The pastor and others were very nice. They were always friendly. However, I never felt a strong connection to anyone.

I got married and life moved forward.

Gabriela helps a student at Sunday school.

All appeared well. Yet my foundation was still broken. Despite my "less than average" attendance at church, the pastor's wife at The Salvation Army would often visit me. She would come to my home, read scripture and pray for me and my family. She spoke of an intimate "one–on–one" relationship that I could have

"I was in a state of loneliness and self-pity when I first met The Salvation Army."

with Jesus. She shared that Jesus was the real foundation for my life. She introduced me to Him. I discovered that I could "stand on Christ, the solid rock."

Today I have built my life upon His foundation, even answering His call into ministry.

Captains Gabriela and Jose Rangel are corps officers.

An Orphan No More
A Place in the Body Of Christ

My life began on the doorsteps of a Korean orphanage as an infant. No doubt, God has carried me through many trials, some at the misguided hands of others; and even more under my own self–induced destructive behavior. I'm not proud of my sinful past, but I'm no longer ashamed of it either; because there's a mediator between the shameful darkness and the justified light.

Lt. Kari Rudd

Jesus' blood shed for my sin, His resurrection for my restoration; to this I cling and for this I rejoice.

And then there's the earthly element of consequence. I had a son with my first husband. The last time I saw my son Kristopher was nearly 14 years ago. Kris was three and we were building Lego houses together. I was building a second one right next to his. He reached over, stopped me, and insisted that we work on one house together. He wanted all of us to live in the same home.

Tough Choice

This is God's desire; that we might all dwell in His heavenly home. I knew this would be the last time I'd see Kris for years to come. In court I'd relinquished all legal rights to child custody. You see, I had been in spiritual warfare, with my son as the pawn. And the devil was winning, in that the pawn was being emotionally ruined.

My reaction was to act as the woman did who was brought before King Solomon when another woman claimed to be the mother of her child. King Solomon settled the dispute by threatening to cut the infant in two. The real mother renounced the child so the infant would live.

I decided to do the same. I knew that Kris would be better off with one parent than torn apart between two families where hatred would prevail; so I let him go out of my great love for him, and with ultimate faith in God.

There remains an ardent ache, a silent sorrow. God wants me to surrender all.

"You're Mine"

About four years ago my husband Eric and I were preliminarily accepted for training as Salvation Army officers. Terrified, of course, I ran from God and stepped back into my sin. I even thought to myself, "I can do this and not feel guilty." And then on a Sunday morning in December, I woke up to the presence of the Holy Spirit. And He was saying, "You're mine!" Subsequently, I confessed and repented; our family was healed and restored.

It took a few rocky years, but God brought us through. God has called me, not because I'm anything extraordinary, but because His love for me is extraordinary. This is my testimony. God's love for me is so immense that even I, an abandoned, foreign born orphan, have been adopted into His forever family, to serve and at times even suffer for His glory. And I do trust that everything is ultimately for His glory.

Lieutenant Kari Rudd was ordained and commissioned as a Salvation Army officer on June 13, 2010 in Cerritos, CA.

Miraculous Call to Ministry
Conversion of a Radical Muslim

I was born to a Jewish Orthodox family and raised in Ethiopia; I converted to Islam at the age of 12. I grew up with a Muslim mother and a Jewish Orthodox father. I came to know the Lord as Savior when I was just 14 years old. The Lord has called me to become a minister. That call is nothing short of a miracle.

I grew up not knowing much about the Bible. I heard that it was forbidden for any common man to read the Bible for himself, unless you were an ordained priest.

Lt. Teddy Beshah

As life got tough, my mother sent me to go to the neighboring country of Kenya to be with my older sister and brother. That is where my life was changed forever.

Before leaving Ethiopia when I was twelve years old, my parents were separated. My mother's side of the family convinced my mother, two sisters and me to become Muslims. They gave some money to my mother and promised her that our lives would change for the better.

Instead, life got harder. My mother sent my older sisters and brother to Kenya to be with her brother. A year later she sent me there to join my siblings.

Refugee

I became a refugee in Kenya, with my sister as my guardian. My uncle is a very radical Muslim who believes in jihad. It did not take long for my uncle to convince me to become a radical Muslim as well. However, the Lord had another plan for me.

I stayed with my uncle because my sister couldn't afford to take care of herself and me. One day I went to visit my sister and I met her Christian friend named Wagaye. She called herself a born again Christian. The lady quickly befriended me, but I hated her for no reason at all. There was something about her that bothered me inside.

Invited To Church

One morning Wagaye asked me if I would join her to go to church. I was not happy about that. She knew I was a Muslim and hated anyone who was not. I was surprised by her audacity. Just out of curiosity, I agreed and went to the church with her.

I remember the peace and the joy I felt that day in that church. Most of all, I appreciated the affectionate love I sensed from the Christians there. After that first visit I became more open toward Wagaye. Two weeks later, she gave me a Holy Bible to read. The next day I read all four gospels in one afternoon.

Changed

The stories I read about Jesus made me believe in Him. I came to believe in Jesus, not just

The lady quickly befriended me, but I hated her for no reason at all.

as a prophet, or only as the son of God, but as my personal Savior and Lord. I began to have a changed mind and heart. Two weeks after that I became a Christian and accepted Christ as my Savior. I became passionate to share my story of new life in Jesus Christ with my family and friends. I was thrown out of my uncle's house and my mother disowned me. Despite the costs and sacrifice, I was certain that the Lord had a bigger plan for my life.

After coming to the United States, I was introduced to The Salvation Army. I had finally discovered God's plan for my future. As I grew in Christ, I developed a genuine passion for those without Christ. My calling became clear. I am grateful to The Salvation Army for giving me, a former Muslim, the opportunity to tell the world about the true, living Savior. Thanks be to God!

Lieutenant Teddy Beshah was ordained and commissioned as an officer in The Salvation Army on June 6, 2010 in Atlanta, GA.

A Marriage Restored
Humility and Forgiveness

I am the oldest of nine siblings. I was born in Mexico and raised by my mother and my stepfather. They loved me and took care of me. I grew up knowing about God and going to church every Sunday.

My stepfather was a hard–working person and a perfectionist. I grew up wanting to be like him, but at the same time I felt insecure and was afraid of being criticized by others if I made any mistakes. I did not recognize this tendency until I became an adult.

Captain Marina Martinez

My stepfather also tried to draw me closer to God. I would do everything I needed to do in church to feel clean of my sins, but the guilt would not go away.

At age 18 I finished my training as a cosmetologist and started working. I thought that by having money I would be successful in life. It seemed that way for a couple of years, but I kept feeling empty. I knew I needed something else besides just going to church. In my search to know who God really is, I met my husband, who guided me to a Christian church where I accepted the Lord as my personal Savior.

In 1991 my husband and I moved to the United States. As I searched for a deeper relationship with God, I met The Salvation Army at the Santa Ana Temple in California. My relationship with God grew deeper. I came to appreciate the value of what Jesus did on the Cross for me.

Take My Life

As time went by my marriage began to collapse. I felt that sometimes my husband and I were like two strangers under the same roof. One day I cried out to the Lord to "give me some of Your love, so I can love."

Months went by and God restored our marriage little by little. But in the process I found out that I could be arrogant at times. I had unconsciously learned from my father that I did not need anything from anyone, so when problems arose in my marriage I would say to myself, "I do not need to ask for forgiveness."

Even with all my defects God still loved me. I did not know how to thank Him for forgiving me and restoring my marriage. With a thankful heart I had the desire to serve Him. I told Him, "Lord I have nothing to give You to thank You enough for what You have done for me. Take my life for Your service."

Job Offers

I was asked to be a part time youth worker at the Santa Ana Temple for a year. Then came an opportunity for me and my husband to lead the Hispanic ministry the San Fernando Valley Corps. We did that for about four years, then spent three years in Santa Ana as corps helper and assistant. Our last appointment was at the Long Beach Temple. From there we were accepted for training as Salvation Army officers.

Making Excuses

At first I tried to excuse myself from having to undergo training and wrestled with God and questioned Him. "Why Lord, why now? My children are too old and one is too young. They are going to have a tough time there. I have hardly any education—just my GED. I really do not like to read and study for long periods of time. My English is not good enough to enter and my husband can barely communicate in English. And besides, we have had success in the ministries that you have put us in. Why God?"

I was trying to make every excuse that crossed my mind not to come to school. I cried and kept questioning God.

The Lord said to me, "It is okay, do not worry."

Everything I have and do is only because God is faithful and is always with me. As Philippians 4:13 says, " I can do everything through Christ who gives me strength."

Captain Marina Martinez was ordained and commissioned as a Salvation Army officer on June 10, 2007 in the Western Territory.

I Put My Rituals Aside
Answering the Call to Ministry

My family came from Laos to the United States in September, 1976. Their journey took them across the Mekong River to Thailand, where my father applied for sponsorship to come to America through the YMCA. We were sponsored by three families in Illinois who attended Good Shepherd Lutheran Church.

Lt. Jean Thammavongsa

I am a first generation American in that I was the first of my family to be born in this country. I was born in Palos Heights, Illinois in 1977 and grew up in the south suburbs of Chicago.

Buddhist Culture

After high school I moved to Rockford with my parents. My family's religion was Buddhist. Even though I grew up in a Buddhist home, I didn't know much about that religion at all. I only knew what to do during the Buddhist ceremonies because of my parents' instructions. No explanations were given as to why we were observing the various Buddhist religious ceremonies. I complied because I accepted that being Buddhist was our culture and I thought that's just what I had to do. It was my parents' belief so I never questioned it and I went through the motions.

It wasn't until 1996, when I met my husband, that I also met Jesus Christ and made Him my Lord and Savior. One might have expected opposition from those in my Buddhist culture, but that was not my experience. My family and friends have been very supportive of my decision to follow Christ.

Since the time of my conversion, God had been using me in children's ministries and ministering to teenage girls. I never thought of it as a calling—it was just something I loved to do. It was not until seven years later that I heard God's call on my life. And in that calling, I understood that this is what I was supposed to be doing for Him.

The Thammavongsa Family

If you had asked me five years ago what I would be doing today, I would never have imagined that I would be a cadet at the College For Officer Training. I was very content with my life at that time. We had our first home, our third child and I had my own styling salon. In addition, I had my own ministry to children and teen girls. What more could I have wanted? Then I met The Salvation Army, and I fell in love with the people there. My family started to attend Rockford Temple Corps where there was a Laotian ministry. We found our place in this "Army" and decided to join it. In 2003 the Rockford Laotian Tabernacle opened and we were enrolled there as soldiers.

God Tugged at My Heart

As I got to know the officers and learned more about The Salvation Army, I felt God tugging on my heart. My corps officer told me that I was "officer material," but I let her words go in one ear and out the other. Then one day, as my husband and I were talking, we confirmed each other's calling. God had been working in each of us, bringing us to the realization that He was calling us to lifetime ministry as Salvation Army officers. With the support of our families and our corps officers, we began the process to enter the training college.

I am a first generation American. I am also a first generation Salvationist and a first generation Salvation Army officer—all because we came and joined the Army!

Lieutenant Jean Thammavongsa was ordained and commissioned as a Salvation Army officer on June 10, 2008 in Des Plaines, IL.

From Russia to the USA
True Freedom for Iron Curtain Family

The Katchanov family used to be known as the Cohens. Sergey knew that, but even his wife Tanya didn't.

Sergey was born in Azerbaijan in 1962. His mother raised him and he didn't meet his father until he was 15.

Sergey, Tanya and their son George were all cadets at Chicago CFOT.

As a child, looking up to the stars at night, Sergey, whose family were atheists, would ask himself, "How could everything have been created if there is no God?" He never discussed this question because God was strictly forbidden in the Soviet Union.

Jewish Heritage

When he was eight years old his mother told him that they were Jewish and that he should never forget his heritage. Although not raised with Jewish traditions, he did absorb some Jewish culture from family friends.

The failure of the Haskalah (Enlightenment Movement) caused many Jewish people to join the Communist Party and the KGB. Sergey's grandfather joined the KGB and eventually changed the family's name from Cohen to Katchanov because of anti–Semitism.

Being poor, the military provided the best career opportunity for Sergey. The military was difficult and he was pressurized by fear. He could not trust anyone. One mistake could mean a prison sentence or worse.

In 1981 he won a military contest and the prize was attendance at a dance. It was there that he met Tanya, whose training allowed her to spend several years as a pharmacist.

She did not know that Sergey was Jewish and her family came from an anti–Semitic background. She later told Sergey that she would never have married him if she'd known he was Jewish. Their marriage was rocky at times and twice they thought about divorce.

Father, mother and son all trained to be officers in Chicago.

Accepting Christ

God had other plans. Sergey, who only heard about Jesus from overhearing old ladies talk about Him, was one day given a tract by Jews for Jesus. This event led him eventually to attend a Jewish music and dance festival that was to feature a famous American preacher. Through the ministry of this festival, Sergey accepted Jesus and began to attend a messianic congregation.

Tanya, an atheist whose grandmother was a believer, was stunned by the change that she saw in Sergey. It frightened her.

Unbeknown to the family, young George, their only son, was being taught Bible stories by Tanya's mother. He actually knew more about Jesus than his parents.

Eventually Tanya attended church with Sergey and she accepted Christ. Much later an opportunity to go to minister together as a family in the United States was presented to the Katchanovs and they accepted. They became involved with outreach work among Russians in Skokie, Illinois, but the denomination sponsoring them couldn't fully support their ministry.

Some years later, a Russian–speaking Salvation Army officer named Ilona Schaal came to their worship service and invited the family to participate in outreach projects for Russian Jews. They visited several Army locations in Chicago and eventually ministered at the Belmont corps there.

While taking soldiership classes, the whole family visited at the College For Officers' Training (CFOT) in Chicago each week. After a year Sergey and Tanya were cadets studying to become ministers in The Salvation Army. George entered the college as a cadet the next year at 19 years old.

Captains Sergey and Tanya Katchanov are stationed in Ghana, West Africa, and their son, Captain George Katchanov, is stationed in Manitoba, Canada.

5 Finding the Way

"Let my teaching fall like rain and my words descend like dew, like showers on new grass, like abundant rain on tender plants."

Deuteronomy 32:2

My Plans, God's Plans
Ready to Face the World

My first real encounter with The Salvation Army took place when I decided to visit Asbury College. Arriving on campus in Wilmore, Kentucky, I discovered that it was also the weekend when prospective students are invited by the Salvation Army Student Fellowship for a preview. I was also shocked when I learned that The Salvation Army is a church.

Carrie McCall

When I came to Asbury as a student, I had no plans to be involved with the Army's Student Fellowship. I came from a United Methodist church and planned to return to the denomination as a children's pastor.

Hanging Out

Things continued this way until my senior year at Asbury. A few of the girls in the Christian Ministries department were Salvationists. We always seemed to end up studying and hanging out in the Sallie Center. Even though I wasn't a Salvationist, Majors Michael and Cathy Himes, the Student Fellowship Directors, always made me feel welcome and loved, and would care for us in practical ways.

During the spring semester Majors hives invited me to go on the spring break mission trip. The price was right and I figured it would be a good trip. During the trip we served in a variety of roles. We did everything from playing timbrels at the Army's Adult Rehabilitation Center to leading the Good Friday service to cleaning the Family Care Center. God started tugging on my heart and I fell in love with the fact that the Army was finding ways to meet the needs of people and share Jesus at the same time.

After the trip, I knew deep in my heart that God wanted me to serve with The Salvation Army, but I pushed it to the back of my heart and mind.

When I graduated from Asbury College two years ago, I didn't have a job. Still, I was convinced that my plans were God's plans. During a long job hunt, I finally started listening to God again. He led me back to the Army.

"God started tugging at my heart."

A Salvation Soldier

Four months after graduating, I accepted a position as an employee with the Louisville–Portland Corps. The following January I was enrolled as a Salvation Army soldier. I'm looking forward to seeing how God uses me and what He has to teach me in this position and future positions with the Army.

Carrie McCall is a soldier at the Louisville–Portland, KY corps.

When the Blessing Came
I Drew a Line in the Sand

On my second Sunday at Asbury College in Lexington, Kentucky I was on my way to a local church when a 15 passenger van passed by. All of a sudden it pulled over and out jumped a short male with curly red hair in full uniform. He called out to me, "Hey, would you like to come with us, Jason?"

I had no idea who he was, and furthermore, I was particularly perplexed as to how he knew my name. In spite of all of this, I decided to accompany them,

Jason Mull

giving the reply, "Yeah, sure," and at that point I still had no idea where I was going. We arrived at the Danville Corps, and I've been hooked on the Army's ministry ever since.

When I arrived at the corps for the first time, I was immediately welcomed with open arms. Once I saw the brass band play I knew I belonged in the Army. Since I am a trombone player, I had longed for a church where my instrument of choice would be used regularly.

What is it that keeps the morale of an army up? Well, it is good music! And I am blessed to be a blessing and to encourage others, as the Lord grants me the ability.

The Uniform Thing

At first I had mixed impressions about the whole uniform thing. The thought crossed my mind that it seemed a bit exclusive, but as time progressed the uniformity began to grow on me as I came to learn what it symbolizes: The sanctified robes of righteousness, set apart to save, saved to serve!

The one thing that truly got me hooked on the Army was the writings of Samuel Logan Brengle. As I read those sacred pages, the scales fell from my eyes. I began to look into the perfect law of liberty that was so plainly spelled out by Brengle. The idea of such freedom from sin had never really occurred to me. If somebody had tried to tell me earlier in my life that it was possible for me to live without sin, I would have laughed in their face and called them a liar. Granted, I had to wrestle with Brengle's Bible–based words for many weeks when I first read his works. But, oh, when the Blessing came, it came in the knowledge of the power of that One who calls me to abide in His presence.

Whose Slave?

For years I had been a slave to the shackles of sin, a slave to the false teaching of defeat for the believer.

The Blessing was a line in the sand, yet it has also been a progressive work. The Master continued to call me higher, quickening me for the journey. I am still not above the wiles of the Devil, but I can stand on the trustworthy foundation of the one I have claimed as my own, the one who loved me first. I am indeed his "Love–Slave" who is owned outright by Love Himself!

Jason Mull is a soldier at the corps in Danville, KY.

A Tug On My Heart
I Didn't Want to Leave. God Said, "Don't."

My association with the Army began when my father, a judge and somewhat well–known figure in my hometown of Marietta, GA joined the Salvation Army Advisory Board. He was impressed with the Army's strong commitment to serving the needy and its unapologetic Christian affiliation.

Taylor Darden

From that point on, The Salvation Army has always been present, off and on, throughout my life. My family began a yearly tradition of ringing bells outside various department stores in our area every Christmas, playing and singing carols. I also volunteered at one Salvation Army day camp in high school, which was exhausting and difficult, but ultimately rewarding.

Surprised

When I began studying at Asbury College, I was surprised to discover the prominence of the Army on this campus. I had no idea. I had not factored this into my college decision. But here I was, at one of the most prominent Salvation Army Student Fellowships (SASF) in the country. Looking back, I would call it a coincidence if I didn't believe in a wise and sovereign God.

My sophomore year I elected to join a mission team to Pittsburgh with the Asbury SASF. Here my eyes were opened to the wealth of ministries the Army offers. I was also pleased to learn the Army's position on giving women equal ecclesiastical rights.

Because it was Holy Week, we were asked to present an Easter service at a particular corps. I ended up giving the sermon!

From then on, I was sold on the Army. I joined the East's Creative Arts Service Team (CAST) just a few weeks later as a last-minute add-on for the group's celebrated summer production of Godspell. (I played John the Baptist.) This ended up being one of the best experiences of my life. I learned that my passion and ability for theatre truly could be used to help others and glorify God; I learned that the arts are important, especially to the church.

I would call it a coincidence if I didn't believe in God.

Toward the end of the summer, I began to feel a strange tug on my heart. I sensed that God was calling me to become a soldier. As I worshipped during one evening of the annual Old Orchard Beach, Maine camp meeting, I remember telling God that I didn't want to leave all of this—all these wonderful people and joyous, service-filled living. It is my belief that He simply replied, "Well, don't."

That was all I needed to hear. I returned to Asbury that fall and began a soldiership class with fellow Asbury students Megan Parker and Christian Loftus. I enrolled in the Lexington, Kentucky Corps this January and am quite happy with my new church. I have no idea where else the Lord will take me in my life, but I'm fairly certain I'll never be far from the ministry of the Army. I believe that everyone should find the best way to serve the Lord, a way that suits them and that God has ordained.

There are countless venues to serve Him. For me, it's The Salvation Army.

Taylor Darden is a soldier at the corps in Lexington, KY.

Time to Take That Step
A New Direction

My first encounter with The Salvation Army was somewhat a selfish one. I had been at Asbury College for almost a year, and was really missing playing in a brass band like I had at home with my dad. The Asbury Salvation Army Student Fellowship (SASF) had a good band. I asked to join, with no other intentions than playing brass music again.

While I had a few friends in the SASF at the time, I still thought the whole Army thing was pretty weird.

Megan Parker

However, after three years of touring with the group, going to Sunday night SASF meetings, taking part in various ministry weekends and reaching out to people, I began to see the real heart of The Salvation Army and what its people are all about.

I became more aware of how those in the Salvation Army live out their love for God and service to others in His name. And an added plus was how the Army provided me with many opportunities to reach out to people by going and doing things in the community with the band. This proved to enrich tremendously my otherwise normal routine as a college student.

Pull on My Heart

I really felt God pull on my heart toward the Army, and when two of my friends said they were going to join I realized it was time to take that step in following God's will for my life.

I approached the corps' Songster Leader Dr. Beatrice Holz, who is professor of Music Education and Voice at Asbury, and explained to her that I felt, after these years of playing with the band, that the Lord was directing me to become a soldier in The Salvation Army. I was enrolled in February, 2009 and graduated that May.

Megan's recital reception

I worked at The Salvation Army's Paradise Valley Camp last summer, and returned to Asbury in the fall to do student teaching. I plan to work toward my Masters Degree in Music while staying in the Lexington area.

I enjoy playing alto horn in the Lexington Corps Band. It is a new adventure and I am excited by what God has in store for me!

Megan Parker is a soldier at the corps in Lexington, KY.

Life Is Not the Same
Walking Up On That Stage Changed Me

"Why are you taking me to a thrift store?" I asked my grandfather, who was employed by The Salvation Army. To my surprise he was bringing me to a youth meeting. The Salvation Army was far more than a thrift store! It was a place full of loving faces and people who accepted me with open arms.

From that evening forward I was at the Army anytime the door was open, and that summer at age nine I was given the opportunity to go to the Army's Camp Happyland.

Lt. Shauntrice Williams

A Void In My Heart

I had a void in my heart that I could not fill, but that summer it was filled with the love of Jesus Christ. From that day on my life was different and I knew I never wanted to turn back.

Throughout my journey as a Christian, God revealed His plan for my life. To my surprise that plan included becoming a Salvation Army officer (minister).

My Heart Stopped

At a youth conference, when I was 14 years old, I felt an unexplainable uncertainty in my mind. The Sunday service that weekend was incredibly good and the sermon was followed by a call to full–time service. I felt my heart stop, my knees trembled and my mouth went dry. I tried to fight standing up but a power within me encouraged me onto the stage and there I was suddenly staring at hundreds of people witnessing my acceptance of a call to the ministry.

My life has not been the same since.

The hardest part of accepting God's call was following through with the decision.

Opportunities

After high school I was given many opportunities to travel the world, make a lot of money and become successful. Upon arriving at Liberty University, I doubted my calling and figured that I could avoid becoming an officer by staying in Liberty's strong Christian environment and pleasing God by becoming a Christian lawyer.

God surprised me again by putting in my heart the desire to become a Salvation Army officer two years earlier than expected. I had just begun a relationship with the man I loved, and would have to leave him behind, along with my family and friends, but that decision was the greatest choice I've made.

My journey to get to where I am today was difficult, but along the way I learned so much about myself and God's unfailing love.

Lieutenant Shauntrice Williams was ordained and commissioned as a Salvation Army officer on June 7, 2009 in Atlanta, GA.

Finding Life, Love, Hope
A Thrill in the Joy of Worship

In January of 1999 I became engaged to a man I had dated on and off for six years. We had finally decided that we were better together than apart, and we wanted to make a permanent commitment to each other. So we needed to find a church we could agree on. Mark had been raised in many different churches, and was not partial to any one of them. I was raised in the church my great–grandparents had courted in, and I knew I did not want to get married there. So we

Captain Stephanie Larrick

asked God for guidance, and started visiting churches. The first Sunday we went to the church Mark's mother attended. Something there did not feel right to me. The second Sunday we went to a different church in the same denomination in which I was raised. My fiancé would have crawled out of his skin if he could have, he was so uncomfortable there.

We Would Know

I knew that he had attended worship services at The Salvation Army when he was in college, and I liked the idea of it, so I asked if we could try there. He agreed. I had said that if God wanted us to stay there, He would show us life, love and hope there. Shortly after we sat down in our pew, we were greeted by a two–year old in front of us named Hope. As we left we were greeted by people like Judy and Karen, who were genuinely glad we were there and really wanted us to come back.

We felt love. So I asked my
fiancé if we could try it again the
next Sunday and he readily agreed.

The third Sunday I had to go
on my own because Mark had to
work, but I knew that was where
God wanted me, so I kept going.

The corps officer (pastor) was
not present for our first few
Sundays due to illness. This was
a good thing because I had an ear

infection at the time, and I'm sure his boisterous guitar playing
would have given me a huge headache. By the time he was back
playing, my ears were ready to handle it. I was actually thrilled
with the idea that worship could be fun.

Control Issues

We attended Bible study there during the week because it fit
better with my fiancé's work schedule. In April of that fateful year
of 1999 I realized that I "had control issues with God," and gave
my life to the Lord. In June we asked the Major to do our wedding
and in November we had a beautiful, Christ–centered wedding.

Then God really started working on us. Christmas Eve of 2000 we
became soldiers (members) and in June of 2004 we became officers
(ministers). But I never would have known the joys and challenges
of officership if God had not shown me that there was hope and
love at The Salvation Army back when we first visited.

Captain Stephanie Larrick is a corps officer.

Singing a New Song
A Crash Course in Salvationism

There they were! Asbury College students who met faithfully each Sunday morning, dressed in dark blue uniforms and with instruments in hand. They would attend a small local corps in the area. This group of students was my first introduction to The Salvation Army! I had grown up in a different church, but found the dedication of these students very appealing. Sometimes I wished for an invitation to go with them. This was really my only contact with the Army until several years later.

Major Annette McInnes

After graduate school, I returned to Asbury College to counsel students and to teach. The person responsible for my getting this position was Salvationist Professor Lee Fisher. We enjoyed working together very much, and 14 months after coming to the campus, Lee and I were married!

New Tunes

Then began my crash course in Salvationism! The first year we were married, we traveled in the U.S. or Canada to preach and teach every weekend. Army music was a struggle for me—there were new songs that had no written music. Some words I knew, but these were sung to a different tune. Often, I recognized the old tunes, but the words were unfamiliar.

After a few embarrassing errors, I learned the rank system. In those days, Salvationists were occasionally "firing volleys and cartridges" and I really didn't know what was happening then!

In the 17 years that Lee and I ministered in the Army, I grew to love, appreciate and strongly support the multi–faceted work of The Salvation Army. The "red, yellow and blue" and all it stands for became an integral part of my life.

Lee's sudden death in 1987 was devastating and my life was shattered. It would have been easy to return to the church I had previously attended, but I felt the Lord was leading me to remain a soldier in the Army.

The Lord's Leading

The opportunity eventually came for me to go as a delegate to the Soldiers' Seminar on Evangelism in Colorado Springs. This provided a wonderful, spiritually refreshing time that I needed.

While there, I met a Canadian officer who had transferred to the Western Territory and who had also lost his spouse. We were both asked to return to the Soldiers' Seminar to serve on the faculty for two years. We enjoyed becoming better acquainted during this time, but could not see how God would lead our lives together. The red epaulets of an officer and my blue soldier epaulets just did not mix!

God had a plan, however, that would unfold in succeeding months. With the approval and support of the Army's top administration, I became an Auxiliary Captain and was appointed to the College for Officer Training staff in the Western Territory. In a short time, I was

The "red, yellow and blue" and all it stands for became an integral part of my life.

promoted to the rank of captain and was then eligible to marry Major Earl McInnes. We could hardly believe the Lord was working this out for us so rapidly!

We continued to serve in the Western Territory until retirement, and have since served several years in post–retirement in pastoral counseling.

God surely does work in mysterious ways in our lives! I am so thankful for all the blessings that have been mine through service in The Salvation Army.

Annette McInnes, who was promoted to Major, is retired and living in Nicholasville, KY with her husband, Major Earl McInnes.

So Many Friends. . .
So Much Reinforcement

I was originally invited to The Salvation Army by a young man whom I was interested in at the time. Upon one of my first trips to the Salvation Army Student Center at Asbury College in Wilmore, Kentucky, I was invited to the Salvation Army Retreat.

I made so many friends in one weekend. I was soon invited to the family dinners on Tuesday nights and to play in the band. The next year my new friends greatly helped with the loss of friends and family members.

Kinzie Pierce

It was impossible for me to walk around campus and not bump into a Sallie friend.

I also met the man I would marry through The Salvation Army.

I decided to become a soldier because I believe I can serve the Lord more through the work of The Salvation Army. The beliefs and practices I learned about lined up with my personal beliefs.

I have made many lifelong friends. I have an unbelievable support system through my brothers and sisters in Christ. I cannot wait to see what the Lord will do through The Salvation Army.

Kinzie Pierce is a soldier at the corps in Danville, KY.

6 Volunteers

"Be strong and courageous, and do the work.
Do not be afraid or discouraged, for the Lord
God, my God, is with you."

1 Chronicles 28:20

A Trip to the City Dump
Reconciling My Heart and Mind

I asked Jesus to be my Savior in July of 1984. I began to attend Colonial Hills Baptist Church in Milford, NH in 1987. It would remain my church home for the next 15 years. It's there that I grew in the Word. There was a strong emphasis taught there on reading and studying the Bible. In addition to the Bible, we drank in the works of Matthew Henry, John Wesley, Eusebius, Josephus, Augustine and Kempis. Though dead, these great Christian minds still speak!

Michael Harper

In 2002, while at the town dump, I stepped into the "still good" shed. I love to read and for years always stopped to look at the old discarded books. That day I happened to see a book entitled "The General Next To God" written by Richard Collier. As I thumbed through it I saw it was about the life of William Booth, Founder of The Salvation Army.

I had heard somewhere that The Salvation Army was "originally" a religious organization. I am ashamed at how I could so quickly make such an uninformed judgment. You see, I realized that all of those years of learning truth alone (as useful as that was) wasn't enough. If all you do is build your faith only upon learning, than it becomes a deformity. It's like a man who has only built up the muscle of his right arm, while allowing the muscles of his left to atrophy.

You need to apply what you learn about God in practical service to God through others. I had become a very unbalanced individual, spiritually speaking.

As I read this book, I was blown away! Why in all of my religious studies had I not been aware of the rich Christian heritage of The Salvation Army? What self–sacrifice! What love! What a God! I was pulled into its pages and gripped by its powerful examples of true Christian service.

Still The Same?

I was humbled. After finishing the book, I decided that I needed to find the nearest Salvation Army and see if it was still the same organization as founded by William Booth. The very next Sunday, I visited the Nashua, NH Corps. I introduced myself to Majors Carl and Barbara Carvill and awkwardly told them I was there because I had found a book at the dump and that it had changed my life, and that I was here and now in essence reporting for duty! Oh how gracious they were to me ... and patient!

After 1 1/2 years of attending church I became a senior soldier and signed my Articles of War. I was employed as the youth worker at the corps for five years. I have learned by God's grace and The Salvation Army that balance in the Christian life is so very important.

The Army life ... That's the life for me going forward, there is no other!

Michael Harper entered the School for Officer Training in the Eastern Territory in 2009.

Discovering the Army
It Started With a War Cry Letter

A letter to the editor in the *War Cry* stated that The Salvation Army is "everywhere" and that the writer had seen it throughout his life.

Roberta Browne

This made me wonder. Either I'd always lived in the wrong place or else I was terribly non–observant. I was 45 years old before I even heard of The Salvation Army. I'm pretty sure I had never seen a Salvation Army sign, or corps, or uniform, nor could I remember ever hearing a bell–ringer at Christmastime.

Move to D.C.

At 45 years old I moved from a small town in the West to Washington D.C. I was having a mid–life crisis and wanted to change my life. This was in the '70s, when a lot of women were experiencing the same thing and were trying to "find themselves." I was not a Christian at the time. It's true I was searching, but I wasn't sure what I was searching for.

D.C. was, indeed, a new life for me. One of the things I wanted to do in the big city was volunteer somewhere. I had become what some would call a "do–gooder." So I looked around for some place to do good. Now remember—I didn't know what I was looking for, and I was not a church–goer.

I really wish I could remember where I first heard about the Army in D.C., but I can't. I do know, however, that in my new do–

gooder mode I looked in the big telephone book, picked several associations and called them. The Army was one. I called SAWSO, which is the Salvation Army World Services Office. The address listed was in downtown D.C., only about seven blocks from where I worked. I thought this would be a good place to volunteer. I asked for information about the Army, and a few days later I got a large envelope containing about half a dozen *War Crys.* I was impressed, both by the quick response and by the magazines themselves. I started reading them and liked what I read. Knowing no different, I headed for the SAWSO office during my lunch hour.

"Keep Going"

It was a cold and rainy March day, and after a few blocks I decided to forget it and just go back to my office, where it was warm and dry. I started to turn around and head back. I'll never forget what happened next. Something said to me, "Keep going." The voice was so clear in my head that I had to obey. I was cold and wet, and I was missing my lunch. But the voice persisted and I bravely went on.

I reached SAWSO and a Salvation Army officer, Colonel Ernest Miller, an angel in disguise, straightened me out about the volunteer idea, told me all about the Army and invited me to his Corps, which I learned for the first time was a church. I didn't know it then, but my search both began and ended at that point.

I ended up volunteering for the Army, but not the way I thought I would. At almost the same time, I found the Lord, found a church home and found a place to "do good." I became a soldier in The Salvation Army a year or so later, and have been one now for 24 years. A few years later, I was even able to introduce my daughter and son–in–law to the Army; they're Majors now!

I know now it was the Lord who told me to "keep going" that cold March day. He has kept me going in The Salvation Army and in His service ever since. And it all started with the "War Cry" of The Salvation Army.

Roberta Browne lives in Cumberland, MD.

A Perfect Opportunity
Serving in the Aloha State

Our roots in Massachu-
setts are deep. So deep that
in 1993 I was asked to run
for the United States Senate.

I am a former Marine
sergeant and Vietnam
veteran, and spent 28 years
in radio broadcasting. My
wife Ann and I also owned
and operated a small
business for 12 years.

We were involved in
ministry for many years
and we both have deep
church roots. In 1986 I

Ann and Gary Todd

experienced the saving grace of Jesus. The Lord led us to an
evangelical church near our hometown, where I served as a deacon,
church chairman and board member for many years. My wife also
served on the church board and was finance secretary for seven years.

Hope For America

My 18 month campaign for the Senate was an extraordinary
experience. Although we did not win the election, I joined with
like–minded people to found an organization called "Hope For
America," which promoted the virtues of honesty, decency, integrity
and morality.

Hawaii

In 2007, my wife and I moved from New England to the Big Island
of Hawaii to be near our daughter and her family. Our son and his

family were soon to follow.

Ann and I have been married more than 40 years, and our two children have given us seven beautiful grandchildren. All are living here in Hawaii.

While Ann was volunteering at a food pantry operated out of a church gym in Waimea, a retired Salvation Army major asked her if she would be willing to run a Salvation Army food pantry for two mornings a week in our new little hometown of Honokaa. She has a heart for those in need. It was a perfect opportunity.

Hearts and Hands

One day in October of 2008, Ann fell and badly injured her foot. She was on crutches for weeks so I offered to step in. It was during the busy holiday season, so I helped prepare for the traditional Thanksgiving Day meals, the kettle drive and the Angel Tree program. I realized that this is a ministry I had been searching for most of my life, and my desire to serve the Lord through The Salvation Army was ignited.

"My desire to serve the Lord was ignited"

In December, 2008, Ann and I became soldiers with the Kona Corps, serving mostly in North Hawaii. We are hoping to become envoys (lay ministers), God willing, but until then we are preparing to serve in any way we can, as we give "our hearts to God and our hands to man."

Gary and Ann Todd are soldiers in the corps in Honokaa, HI.

Victorious Volunteers
Bringing God's Purpose Into Focus

Who would have guessed that volunteering at a funeral parlor would lead to a path of life service as one of God's workers in The Salvation Army?

Well, that is what happened. Sounds strange, but it's true. My husband Joel and I first came into contact with The Salvation Army in Joliet, Illinois, while trying to find a place to volunteer our services. It was Christmastime, and Majors Garry and Nancy Lowder were the officers in charge. They had the use of a funeral parlor, two blocks away from our apartment as a station to set up for the annual Christmas campaign to help the needy and hurting.

Lt. Etta Johnson

We had just moved to Joliet from Chicago. We have always been keen on volunteering, so we went searching for a place to help and ended up at The Salvation Army. We were members at another church, but Joel's work schedule made it hard for him to attend services. So he began attending services at The Salvation Army.

God's Desire

During this time so many things were happening that made us think that God wanted to use us beyond our occupying a corner at church. I began reading a book that had sat on our shelf for years, Rick Warren's Purpose Driven Life. Some of the things in it kept coming back to my mind. One evening Joel was switching channels and a pastor was speaking about the different areas of the body of

Christ and how they worked together to serve God in different ways. What he said about The Salvation Army's contribution rang true to what we felt God wanted from us. Soon we ended up attending services at The Salvation Army together.

Majors Garry and Nancy Lowder invited us to attend the Commissioning Service of 2007, where cadets who have undergone training are ordained as Salvation Army officers. When the call for officership was given while Joel and I were praying, I felt that God was drawing us to serve Him in this capacity. We accepted the call and told God if it was His will for us we would serve Him in this way.

"We have always been keen on volunteering, so we went searching for a place to help."

Soon after this, God started opening the doors to attend the College for Officer Training.

It was something we never thought we would be doing. Our greatest desire has always been to serve God in any way He wants us to, and we had a heart to help His people. God truly showed us that He had a purpose for us both to do, for His glory, in The Salvation Army.

Lieutenant Etta Johnson was ordained and commissioned as a Salvation Army officer on June 13, 2010 in Schaumburg, IL.

Faith in Action
Keeping the Flame Afire in Appalachia

The great Salvationist song-writer, Sidney Cox, once penned these words—"He sought me, He sought me, when I was wandering far away; He found me, he found me, O what a wonderful day!" Such phrases often conjure up ideas of an individual who has been gloriously saved from a wretched life of sin. Yes, I too can relate to these words, but if you are anxious to read about a scandalous life of sin, you will be quite disappointed.

Lt. David Costellow

At one point in my life, I felt that I had no significant testimony because I became a Christian at a very young age and never got involved in what we often refer to as the "wrong crowd." At the age of 13, I was confident that God was calling me to what is known in many religious circles as "the ministry." Although I had no clue as to what that would look like, I obediently followed that calling by taking full advantage of opportunities to minister in various settings over the next several years.

Urgency

Throughout those years of ministry, I continually felt a deep sense of urgency to have a ministry that was both social and spiritual in nature, but I was never able to find a venue where both were properly administered. The words of James 2:17 constantly troubled me: "In the same way, faith by itself, if it is not accompanied by action, is dead." I often asked God, "If this is the kind of ministry that you desire for me, why can't I find a church that is as concerned with social needs as they are with spiritual ones?" However, I never gave up; I continued to seek God's ultimate calling for my life.

One day, after being tired of searching, the Lord used The Salvation Army to find me. At the time, the Appalachian town that I was ministering in had been devastated by a flood. Through that tragedy, God used a Salvation Army canteen along with a divisional disaster services director to spark a flame in me that has not since died. At the time I had no idea what The Salvation Army was, other than that it was a Christian organization. The ministry I observed that day drew me to what they were doing.

> **God used a Salvation Army canteen to spark a flame in me**

I soon began corresponding by telephone with an officer at the Southern Territorial Headquarters who informed me of the many facets of Salvation Army ministry, including the fact that they are a church. Like William Booth, I had finally "found my destiny!" What a truly wonderful day it was!

Paul told the church at Philippi, "Being confident of this, that He who began a good work in you will carry it on to completion until the day of Christ Jesus." God is carrying out the ministry that He began in me as a teenager in my service for God and man as a Salvation Army officer.

Lieutenant David Costellow was ordained and commissioned as a Salvation Army officer on June 8, 2008 in Atlanta, GA.

Unsafe Friends
A 12-Step Bible Study Changed My Life

Thieves, liars, users . . . As a teenager, I did not choose my friends wisely. My friends were troublemakers, much to the dismay of my parents. We smoked cigarettes, shoplifted, smoked pot and skipped school.

Captain Julie Feist

I was not a happy person and I was addicted to unsafe people. I knew my lifestyle was not good. I knew about God, but Satan and my so–called friends convinced me that God was not interested in me.

As a young adult, I continued to seek out unsafe people and ended up in an abusive relationship in October of 1992.

Hearing Testimony

In May of 1995, I got brave and left that relationship and moved back home with my parents. Two days later, my father invited me to a 12–step Bible study, which I attended reluctantly. At this meeting, a woman shared her testimony. She told us of a life filled with bad choices and of shame. I felt an instant connection. She told us someone had given her a Bible while she was in jail and there she discovered the love and grace of Jesus Christ. She told us she gave her life to Him, and now her life was no longer hopeless.

The Serenity Prayer

After that meeting, while praying the serenity prayer, I asked

God to take over my life.
I knew I could no longer
live the way I had been
living. I immediately
began to feel a sense of
peace, and a tremendous
burden lifted. My life
began to change that very
night. I could tell, and so
could my parents.

Since then, the Lord has
been actively working in my life. I began to study His word, and to
seek His will. He showed me I was worthy of safe relationships. He
opened the door for me to work for The Salvation Army, where I
could also worship. He showed me I was His child and valuable.
My life suddenly had purpose. Every step I took in faith, God called
me into a deeper commitment.

Ground Zero

In 2001, I went to New York to help with the relief effort at
Ground Zero. It was there God revealed His plan for my life. He
called me to be a Salvation Army officer. The same God, who Satan
once convinced me had no interest in me, called me to serve Him
for the rest of my life.

Captain Julie Feist and her husband, Major Larry Feist, are corps officers.

A Deeper Walk
From Sales to Service

I grew up in a non–denominational church in Ohio, where I accepted Jesus as my Savior at age 11, attended every youth function I could and learned much about the Bible. In 1996 I went off to Grove City College in Pennsylvania, and it was there while attending a local Assembly of God church that I really grew in my relationship with Jesus.

Also, I met my future wife while at college. Immediately after graduation we were married and started our family in Northeast

Lt. Jason Brake

Ohio. We attended an independent church called the Community of the Crucified One, where I learned about a deeper walk with and commitment to God.

Early in 2005 we felt the Lord leading us as a family to move from Ohio to Vermont. So I ended my career in sales and marketing with a large industrial supply company and we packed up a truck and headed to Northern New England. This was the first step in my coming to The Salvation Army. The only experience that I'd previously had with The Salvation Army was when I was young and my father had been laid off and we received some food from a corps.

Camp

I met the officers of the corps in Barre, Vermont at my mother–in–law's Bible bookstore. They were regular customers of this store

where my wife was working.
Captain Patrick took an interest in
me personally and in the spring of
2005 I found myself driving the van
as a volunteer to Youth Councils at
Camp Sebago in Maine with the
kids from the Barre Corps. As the
days went by, I was increasingly
involved in many activities at the
corps. I really fell in love with the
work of the Army while on staff at
Camp Sebago. Today, I know for

sure that my call to officership in The Salvation Army is what I am
supposed to be doing with my life.

Recently, I have been learning not to rely on my own strength
and abilities in the undertaking of my tasks. It is comforting to
know that Christ is with me in this adventure.

Grace

Why did God choose me for this work? I'm definitely not a
perfect person, but I think it has to do very much with divine grace.

I believe even more now than I did just a couple of years ago,
that Jesus has called me to share with others the truth of His love
and forgiveness. I also have come to trust that He has called me to
be a minister and to do His good works within The Salvation
Army. I am really excited to see all that the Lord has in store for me
in the coming days and look forward to each coming opportunity.

Lieutenant Jason Brake was ordained and commissioned as a Salvation Army officer
on June 14, 2009 in White Plains, NY.

Simplicity and Humility
Fulfilling the Great Commission

We served as missionaries, teachers and pastors in Hong Kong from June 2006 to August 2007. The Lord led us to come back to the United States and we settled in the Fort Collins, Colorado area.

For a long time we were dissatisfied with church life. It seemed the church in general was very insular and self–centered. In Hong Kong we were drawn to minister to people in great need— people in our village and refugees. Most churches we encountered

Barry and Kirindi Goldman

did very little work to reach out and meet the spiritual and social needs of the surrounding community. We find this to be true both in the U.S. and Hong Kong.

While we were in Hong Kong my wife completed her B.Th. at the United Wesleyan Graduate Institute. We met a few Salvation Army officers there but thought no further about it.

Spirits Resonate

When we arrived in Colorado, we began to look around for ministry opportunities in the local churches. I wrote to many ministries, including the local Army corps in the phone book. I wrote to the captain. He was the only one who responded to any of my email inquiries. He invited me to come and visit and I did.

We began to fall in love with the simplicity, humility, sincere worship and service to the community that we saw there. Then I read a book about the history of The Salvation Army in China. That really fired me up. We were very inspired by the self–sacrifice and genuine discipleship portrayed as we read this book. I then read the biography of William Booth. His teachings on holiness and evangelism resonated with our spirits.

We quickly came to the decision that we wanted to serve the Lord in The Salvation Army. I am now serving as the music director of the Fort Collins Corps.

True Discipleship

In our entire Christian life we have not found any other church or organization that was truly fulfilling all the instructions and commands of the Lord Jesus in the spirit of true discipleship. Each church we have been to fulfills part of the commission, but The Salvation Army seems to us to have a more comprehensive vision and program.

I thank God for the opportunity to be disciples of Christ through the balance of spiritual salvation and social salvation that The Salvation Army offers the world.

Dreams of Revival

Our passion is to be fully committed to a lifestyle of prayer and worship of God and service to man. We want to see the spirit of revival that was personified by our founder, General Booth, flourish in this area. We want to see an army of intercessors with servant hearts established in our corps.

We have dreams of evangelizing the local Colorado State University campus. We want to inspire college age men and women, as well as university professors, to become a part of the "Army without guns." We hope to appeal to the longing that God has placed in these people to live for something more than themselves, to embrace the principles of selflessness and the cross of Christ.

Our captain has charged me with developing a Community School for the Arts to serve the surrounding area. We hope, by establishing personal relationships with people in our community, that we will demonstrate the love of Christ and draw them into the saving knowledge of the Lord.

We are passionate to have people experience the truth of "tasting the Lord and seeing that He is good."

We are passionate about tearing our minds away from the attractions of the world and bringing every thought captive and obedient to Christ. We want to share this passion with everyone we meet.

Barry and Kirindi Goldman live in Fort Collins, CO.

7 Hand to Man

"Blessed are the merciful, for they will be shown mercy."

Matthew 5:7

Another Chance
Soaring for the Lord

I was born in Caguas, Puerto Rico and came to the United States with a purpose in 2003. My life is driven by a passion to serve God with all my spirit, mind and soul.

On December 27, 2003 I left Puerto Rico determined to become an airplane mechanic. I attended the Spartan School of Aeronautics in Tulsa, Oklahoma. I met my future husband and we married ten months later. My pastor warned me about my wrong decision regarding

Eva L. Morales

marriage, but I didn't follow his advice. Instead I delayed my study plan and am now suffering the consequences.

I then moved to Spartanburg, South Carolina, where I became a pastor of the Upper South Carolina Conference of the International Holiness Church. I studied in a Missionary Bible Institute. The van I had purchased for the church was destroyed by a drunk driver. A fellow church member was injured in her right eye. Thanks to the grace of God she recovered.

We then moved to Pompano Beach so I could attend American Flyers flight school. Three months later, we relocated to Forth Worth, Texas where I continued my education with American Flyers.

Discovery

I stayed in Fort Worth for three months and discovered my husband had been abusing my children. I moved to San Antonio,

Texas with my children. We spent three days in a motel and called the crisis line. They provided us the phone number for the Hope Center Emergency Family Program. We stayed there for two months and 19 days.

Hope

With the help of Captains Wanda and Marvin Trayler, we found hope, love and understanding. They invited us to dinner and to attend two different churches, their ministry and the Southside Corps Hispanic Ministry. The Work Force (WIA) Program provided me the financial assistance to continue my education. Mr. Sergio Perez, the career development specialist, has been a blessing in my life. He continues to offer me professional advice and outstanding services. At present, I am studying at the southwest campus of St. Philips College. Professors Rafael Brisita, Rodney Cotter, Hector Ramos, Roland Ward, Juan Guarnero, Mr. Ray and all the staff are outstanding!

Flying for God

God opened doors and gave me a second chance to accomplish my goals. I am also participating in the Scattered Sites Transitional Housing Program of The Salvation Army.

My next goal is to build a traditional experimental airplane of wood and fabrics and dedicate it to God. It will be used to conduct missionary trips to Mexico, the Caribbean and Latin America.

Eva L. Morales lives in San Antonio, TX.

Our Very Own Service
Back Into the Fold

When my job as office manager in the timeshare department of a resort and conference center was discontinued, I knew that a lot of changes were going to take place . . . although I never knew just how many parts or how much of my life they would affect.

Penny Harrison

The unemployment checks were barely enough to cover our bills and not much more. Getting desperate, we began to go once a month to the Salvation Army food pantry. Donna, the pantry worker, invited us to a Friday night free meal and music night called "7th Step." We went, figuring it would be a night out of the house that wouldn't cost us anything and with food and entertainment included.

God's Hand

We were surprised when a yellow flyer was handed out asking us, "Do you have a church home?" We had recently had a very bad—almost shunning—experience from a local church and we were reluctant to attend anywhere else. But that was God's hand, in the most unlikely and unbelievable place, working to bring me and my family back into the fold.

We came that first Sunday as a small way of showing our gratitude to The Salvation Army for what they had done and continued to do for our family. We came in and were greeted by an unusual sight—a group of worshippers turning their faces in welcome toward us. They smiled and greeted us all, meeting our eyes and shaking our hands. They didn't know that those small acts of welcome did so much more—they melted the ice that had unknowingly surrounded my heart during the past few years.

The adult Sunday school and the worship service that followed seemed to have been planned specifically for us. When the opening scenes of "Open the Eyes of My Heart" hit the screen, I felt like Jesus was saying, "Welcome home."

The next week was a flurry as we all looked forward to the following Sunday. It didn't take long for my need to "help" to take over, which grew into a friendship with Captains Shelley and Trevor McClintock and eventually led me to enroll as a soldier (senior members of the church).

As the captains and the others can now tell you, God's hand is evident in every part of my life … I also find evidence of His hand in their lives too! All the changes, even the loss of my job (which I hated so much at the time), was a blessing from God, opening the opportunity of Sunday worship to us. Previously, since I worked every Sunday, I couldn't attend church. My new job, which I found shortly after starting to attend The Salvation Army, allows for flexibility and works well with my duties as a church leader.

Penny Harrison lives in Manitowoc, WI.

Rescued
Met With Open Arms

I didn't grow up under the best of circumstances. By the time I was 11 years old, I was helping my mother raise my two younger brothers. We had always shopped at Salvation Army thrift stores, but I never knew that they offered other services. That all changed in the winter of 2002, when my four–year–old son and I became homeless.

Rose Howard

After Two Years

Since we had no family, we ended up staying at a gospel mission in Modesto, California. The Salvation Army helped us get clothing and shoes.

Eventually, we found ourselves at the Salvation Army homeless shelter in Jefferson City, Missouri, where my car broke down in the parking lot.

The people at The Salvation Army accepted us without any questions. We stayed there for three months and were able to get a new start after more than two years of being homeless. We had been in our apartment about three months when Major Ben Stillwell called me and asked me if I would put in my application for the shelter monitor position.

I was hired in November 2004. Major Beth Stillwell started talking to me about joining the Women's Ministries group. I was a little hesitant at first because I didn't know what to expect. I don't have any sisters and my mother wasn't really a strong female figure in my life, so I didn't know how to act around a group of women, especially women who were mostly older than me, but Major Beth kept inviting me. She knew how much I enjoyed crochet and needle point, and how important it is to be with others who share your interests.

Means Everything

The first meeting I attended was a little stressful, but I was accepted with open arms. I began to feel right at home. I came to the meetings every week until I was hired as the corps secretary.

Because of my job, I don't get to attend the meetings very often now, but I do get the chance to pop in from time to time to see how things are going. I do get to attend the scrapbooking meetings on Tuesday nights.

The Salvation Army means almost everything to me. They rescued me and my son from the harsh life of the streets and gave us food, clothing and a roof over our heads. They offered me a job when I had no prospects, then the Women's Ministries programs and Home League ladies gave us a family. Now I think of these women as my mothers, aunts, sisters, and even daughters in some cases, but mostly I think of them as friends.

Rose Howard lives in Jefferson City, MO.

Three Meals And a Cot
Losing My Life to Gain It

"Is this what life has to offer?" Those thoughts ran through my head one morning as I woke up in the back of a pickup truck with all of my possessions around me.

I started life growing up in an alcoholic, single parent home, for most of my childhood. From there I gained my independence at the age of 18 and started what would be my own 12–year downward spiral with drugs and alcohol. I went from maintaining good jobs and friends to having none at all. Each year that went

Lt. James Curry

by something seemed to get stripped from my life.

Bad Turn

This, of course, was nobody's fault but mine. Life took a particularly bad turn when I finally lost everything I had, except for a few items I carried in bags with me.

Life on the streets was unfamiliar, but necessary for me to continue to feed my addiction. Some days I had nothing to eat except a pound of sugar for my three meals.

That life gets tiring and lonely. People walk by you like you are not there; it seems they are afraid and want nothing to do with you. When the morning would come I'd ask myself, "Is this what life has to offer? Am I going to die or not?" I guess I just got tired of living day by day not knowing what was going to happen. So I went to a county agency looking for homeless shelters and they gave me a sheet with several agencies listed. I went outside, dug into my pocket and pulled out my last quarter.

Rehab

I had a big decision to make. What agency would I choose? I looked up and down the list and saw The Salvation Army. I have to admit I knew nothing about the Army, but my mind urged

me to call them. After debating for a while, I called and they told me they had a drug program. It lasted six months. All I needed to do was work eight hours a day and go through the program. I thought: "For three squares and a cot I will do anything."

That is how I met the Army and accepted Jesus Christ into my life more than 13 years ago. My questions about what life has to offer were answered through the love of good officers and volunteers.

Giving Back

I decided to dedicate myself to giving back to the church that helped me in my time of need. Although I've made a few mistakes along the way, I have kept that promise. I intend to keep that promise until God calls me home.

One lesson I learned early on is found in Romans 12:2: "Do not conform any longer to the patterns of this world, but be transformed by the renewing of your mind. Then you will be able to test and approve what God's will is: His good, pleasing and perfect will."

Lieutenant James Curry was ordained and commissioned as a Salvation Army officer on June 14, 2009 in Merrillville, IN.

Living Water
A Bottomless Well

My husband and I often joke that our children grew up and we left for college. We have four children. Jacob, our youngest, is now 20 years old. The year he graduated from high school, we came to the Salvation Army School for Officer Training. I was saved when I was 11, but it wasn't until I found the Army that I began to seek my purpose in Christ.

I was introduced to the Army while I was working as a neighborhood executive for the Boy Scouts of America. My job was to

Lt. Susan Thwaite

offer a scouting program to youth in "at risk" neighborhoods. One part of my job was to network with area agencies and churches to help meet the needs of these young people. Since The Salvation Army and the Boy Scouts have a national agreement for offering scouting programs as an option for boys' groups, together we made a great team and positively influenced many young lives.

Seeing Christ

I knew nothing about the Army at the time except that they helped people at Christmas. I was pleasantly surprised to learn that they did so much more. I quickly learned that it was a church that often helps those who are less fortunate in our communities. Working with the Army, I could see Christ in the ministry of the officers, who had the ability to touch lives and give hope to so many. I had never been part of a church that actually worked with the poor, lonely and lost.

It didn't take long for my husband, Joel, and me to begin attending the Washington, Pennsylvania Corps. We started by going to Bible study, quickly grew into attending holiness meetings and then Sunday school. We went from attending church only occasionally to never missing a meeting.

The Army gave me a thirst for God. I felt like I couldn't get enough of Him.

My husband and I soon became soldiers and took on local officer positions in the corps, with my husband as the Corps CSM and

"The more we thirst, the more He gives."

myself as the Young Peoples CSM. We were finally living our faith!

I thought I had finally found my purpose in Christ, but He had more surprises in store for us both; I was learning that God continually grows us. The more we thirst, the more He gives. My husband and I attended the Candidates' Seminar (to learn about training to become Salvation Army officers) on two different occasions. It was during our last visit to the School for Officer Training that my husband and I both received the same message from God. We were to wait until our son graduated from high school and then come to Training School. This gave us two years to prepare ourselves to fulfill the calling that God had placed on our lives.

I am excited to see what God will do next. While I do not know what the future holds, I do know Who holds the future.

Lieutenant Susan Thwaite was ordained and commissioned as a Salvation Army officer on June 6, 2010 in White Plains, NY.

God Is Enough
He Will Lead Me

Prior to my commitment to The Salvation Army, I spent a significant amount of time church shopping. I was searching for the right body of believers whom I felt best answered God's purpose for the church.

Lt. Marquis Brookins

The Salvation Army has done a fine job of answering the great commission. However, the aspect of ministry that attracted me to The Salvation Army most is the emphasis it placed on its social services.

The Salvation Army feeds the hungry, satisfies the needs of the thirsty, takes in strangers, clothes the naked, cares for the sick and visits the imprisoned. Most importantly, The Salvation Army encourages the community to share in social service opportunities. This reality is what drew me to The Salvation Army and led me to make the Army my home.

Doing God's Work

Those who are in The Salvation Army know that it is easy to stay busy working for the Lord. Although I am a first generation Salvationist, I promptly learned this fact. As I began to share in the responsibility to first minister to and then care for those in need, I spent more and more time away from home. As my family noticed my absence, they began to question me about my corps involvement. The simple response I shared with my loved ones was, "There is work to be done for the Lord and His people, and we need more help."

In response, my family also began donating their time and their abilities to assist in corps activities. Now my extended family members are Salvationists—ready and willing to serve.

Lts. Marquis and Twyla Brookins

The most significant event that has occurred in my life over the last few months is an ongoing revelation of who God is and who I am. The longer I live, the more I learn that God is enough for me today and tomorrow. With every new glimpse of His glory I realize that I am slowly letting God out of the tiny, tinted box that I had placed Him in. The most important revelation is that God will meet me where I am and take me to where he wants me to be.

I am fearfully and wonderfully made. God is daily revealing to me small fractions of His plan to give me and my family a hope and a future. I have been saved by the blood of Jesus. I have accepted God's call to ministry. My family and I are moving forward— pressing on toward the goal to win the prize for which God has called us heavenward in Christ Jesus.

God is personal, intimate, and powerful; yet He has the capacity to reveal Himself simultaneously to a whole body of believers. And He is working through The Salvation Army. Be a part of it. Come Join Our Army!

Lieutenant Marquis Brookins was ordained and commissioned as a Salvation Army officer on June 8, 2008 in Chicago, IL.

30 Years, $100 a Day
Saved by a "Rush of Wind"

I struggled for years with many addictions, all starting with alcohol. Wanting something stronger, I started to use cocaine. Soon that was not enough for me. Eventually I became an IV drug user. This insane addiction lasted for about 30 years. I lost my family and friends in exchange for a habit that cost me $100 a day. I had become the worst of the worst. I was involved in street gangs dealing drugs. I went to any length necessary to protect this habit of destruction.

Brian Smith

One day I packed up and moved to Florida. I thought I was making a new start, but I brought my drug habit with me. The money that was going to give me a new life lasted about two months.

Too Powerful

I ended up sleeping under bridges and in abandoned cars and houses. A gas station owner let me sleep inside his station if I cleaned the store and stocked the shelves … it didn't take me long to ruin that privilege. I could not hold down a job, my addiction was too powerful. It was a vicious cycle … the result of 30 years of reckless living and many near–death experiences. This had to stop.

With nowhere to go, I went to

When you're the "worst of the worst" is rescue possible?

the Salvation Army Men's Shelter
in Orlando for a free night's rest
and something to eat.

God Was Waiting

One day, I fell on my knees and
cried out to God: "Please take this
taste for drugs out of my mouth." For
some reason I went back to the Men's
Shelter as a volunteer. I overheard
someone talking about the Army's
Adult Rehabilitation program

(ARC) a few miles away. I went to check it out and I was accepted.

I realize now that God has answered my prayer. God was there
all that time, just waiting for me to come running into His loving
arms to be rescued. I repented and 1 Peter 5:6 was brought to my
attention: "Humble yourselves, therefore under God's mighty
hand, that He may lift you up in due time."

I met a wonderful man at the ARC named Major Cortland
Moore. He was a godsend … he showed me how much God loves
all of us. I started to do Bible studies and learned about a wonderful new way of life. Incredibly, God even gave me the strength to
stop smoking cigarettes as well.

Doing Right

With God's help, I became an alumni of the ARC program and
an adherent member of the Salvation Army Corps in Orlando. I
started looking for work and prayed for guidance. My old boss
from the gas station asked me if I was looking for work. Our God
is a God of miracles … after all I did to this man, he accepted me
back. As he noticed the change in me, he gave me a full time job
and then promoted me to manager. God is good!

With God's help, I bought a computer and contacted my three
sisters. I had not seen them in 17 years. One month later, one of my
sisters died of breast cancer. She had been sick for a long time and I

firmly believe that God kept her alive to know that her brother was sober.

I was sober for two years when I saw an old friend of mine. As I was on my way to party with him, this wind rushed in front of me, making me think of what I was about to throw away. The wind of the Holy Spirit caused me to go back to my room.

Now, six years later, I am the chaplain at the Men's Shelter, preaching the Word of God to others who also battling addictions. Now I am able to give back what the Lord gave to me.

Brian Smith lives in Orlando, FL.

I Had It All
A Faceless Man Fights His Way Back

At the age of 31, I was an international banker; the senior vice president of a Canadian bank, overseeing the multi–billion dollar portfolios of nine U.S. financial institutions ... I had it all! I was on top of the world and could make and break the rich and famous with the stroke of my pen. Until, that is, my wife announced over drinks and dinner at our favorite restaurant just as the sun was going down over the purple bay that our love was a lie and our marriage was over.

Dominic Mance as a young man

Then I received a phone call from the bank telling me that they had filed for bankruptcy. I lost everything—my beautiful wife and two precious daughters, my prominent job, my flashy black car with the tinted windows and my palatial home near the sea—it all disappeared before my very eyes, like a pencil line on a piece of paper quickly erased. I became a homeless vagabond overnight. I came in contact with The Salvation Army when I was living on the streets. They were serving bag lunches to homeless and needy people like me five days a week.

Soul Burning Down

Once a person of sober responsibility, I began wandering from place to place, drinking like a very thirsty man and smoking enough cigarettes to burn down my soul. Then in the dead of night, as the cigarettes and cheap booze oozed from my pores and

I felt what I can only describe as perfect misery, I considered ways to end my life. But a still, small voice seemed to say, "If you just prevail, someday you will feel perfect joy." I held onto that promise; I held on tight …

Throughout all those hard scrabble, knock–about years on the street of broken dreams, I stayed in libraries during the day and seedy bars at night and slept in old cars or on somebody else's couch. I lived a million different lives, in a million different ways, trying to forget, trying to remember, trying to forget again. I tried my hand at all kinds of trades, too, and sometimes worked three or four odd jobs all at the same time that always led to the same old, dead–end street.

I was a faceless man without an identity … I tramped a million miles to hell and back, ever–searching, never finding and forever running away. I was a good–for–nothing, broken–down money machine trying to figure out how to become a living, breathing human being. So I read countless books looking for answers to questions that I didn't even know how to ask.

Invisible Friend

I recognized early on, though, that there was this invisible "something" taking care of me; and after a series of chance meetings with The Salvation Army, whose members, at first, seemed to me to be certifiably nuts, I began reading the Bible and praying a lot. Eventually I came to the realization that that indefinable "something" was the person of Christ.

About six months later, I surrendered my life to Him and God gave me a heart for the homeless and a gift for writing; but I was so broke that I used those stubby, yellow pencils they had at the library I hung out at; and I wrote my stories on the back of colorful flyers that were red, yellow, green and blue, just like beautiful balloons.

I began typing and submitting my work to publishers from a smoke–filled, cockroach–infested halfway house for the homeless reeking of pesticide that I called my home away from home …
And my work was getting published!

Some years later, I discovered, much to my surprise, that I could draw; and within a year, my art was appearing in galleries. And, if that's not enough, all by the grace of God, I'm also now a songwriter/singer and radio broadcaster. And my life story has been dramatized by the "UNSHACKLED!" radio program and heard around the world.

In time, I came to realize that even though we might have big homes, fancy cars and important jobs, we're just like homeless tramps on the inside because we have poor, hungry souls. I want to tell the world what Jesus Christ has done in my life, to help the countless people wasting their lives pursuing those foolish, superficial dreams like I once did, trying to get what I had but lost.

God will never leave you or forsake you and His promises are faithful and true. This is a story which must be told; so now, I've told it to you.

Dominic Mance attends the Salvation Army corps in Redondo Beach, CA.

8 Many Walks of Life

"Come, all you who are thirsty, come to
the waters; and you who have no money,
come, buy, and eat!"

Isaiah 55:1

Never Too Late
To Embrace Holiness

When I was a boy at youth meetings and Bible camps, I felt the Lord calling me to serve Him.

In high school I was a stock clerk at J.C. Penney's in a small town in South Dakota. The window display lady there introduced me to The Salvation Army.

Later, while I was in the Marines, two fellow marines told me how to be saved. I accepted Jesus Christ as my Savior from sin and as the Lord of my life.

After being discharged from the service, I felt called to attend The

Norbert Limmer

Bible Institute of Los Angeles to become a Wycliffe Bible Translator in South America. I signed up to go, but my parents objected. So I didn't do it.

A College Decision

At college, I signed up for pre-seminary training. I had a hard enough time with English, so Hebrew and Greek did not work for me.

After marrying and having four children, I had a vision to become a Baptist minister. I checked out Baptist seminaries, but never followed through.

Having majored in art, Jesus urged me in my later years to do more spiritual painting. So I've been doing that ever since, and I felt called to join The Salvation Army to serve Him more fully in other ways also. I became a soldier last September at the age of 81.

Now with five grown children, six grandchildren and my wife

gone on to glory, I'll see what adventures Jesus has ahead for me, but I wonder still "what could have been."

Holiness

I often recall with fondness my earlier years working with a former "Army Lassie" whose whole life was one of

Norbert with his five children and six grandchildren.

holiness. I wanted that same for me, my family and others.

Praise God, it's never too late.

Norbert Limmer lives in Minneapolis, MN.

Not Just a Thrift Store
God Knows My Name

When growing up, I always thought that The Salvation Army was just a thrift store. I used to ask myself, "Why would my mother give birth to me in a thrift store?"

It wasn't until many years later that I understood that I wasn't born in a Salvation Army thrift store, but in a Salvation Army hospital, Booth Memorial.

My birth mother did not want me and she tried several times to abort me, but I guess God had other plans for me in this world. With no other options available to

Helen Hicks

her, my mother stayed at the Army's Booth Memorial Hospital for the remainder of her pregnancy and that's where I was born, and then given up for adoption.

I was raised in a decent family. From an early age my parents told me I was a special child given to them by the grace of God.

Addiction

My adoptive parents separated when I was 13, and I chose to live in the city with my dad.

Six months after moving to the city, I was introduced to cocaine. For the next 16 years cocaine became my life.

My story in some ways is not much different from others who have struggled with drug and alcohol addiction. During my years of addiction I was brutally raped by a caretaker on my mother's property. I was involved in a number of abusive relationships. I stole over $100,000 from my mother and I was in and out of jail from the age of 17.

Attempted Murder

I tried to murder the man who had molested my own son. I remember the night clearly. I went into the bedroom with a loaded gun, put the barrel of the gun to his head and pulled the trigger. But nothing happened. I ran outside and shot the gun up into the air and it went off.

By 1997, I was sitting in jail waiting to go to prison. I had been sentenced to 14 years.

My First Prayer

For the very first time in my life I got on my hands and knees and cried out to God to help me. The next morning I was called to the front of the jail cell block, thinking I was about to go to prison. But I was told, "You're going back to court."

The court was lenient and I was released after nine more months in jail and sent to a program for addicts. Since that day I have never used drugs, and I have never gone back to jail.

Openly Welcomed

I am grateful to The Salvation Army. Perhaps because I was born at the Army's Booth Memorial, I was openly welcomed the first day that I walked into one of their church services.

I wasn't only welcomed, eventually I became a senior member of the congregation (a soldier). I also got married in The Salvation Army and later I was given an opportunity to work for the Army as well.

Today, with over ten years of being clean and sober, I live a free life.

God had a plan for me to be on this earth. The Salvation Army helped me turn my life around and it brought me back home.

Helen Hicks lives in southern California.

Long Road Back
From Sorcery and the Hell's Angels

Although I was raised in a Catholic family, I became a witch, lived with the Hell's Angels, became a Christian and moved into a Christian commune—all by the time I was 19.

Chuck and Dorothy Sapp

The commune kicked me out after a year, but a seed was planted. I tried several churches over the years, but I always found a reason to stop going. I would get back into drugs and get further and further away from God.

Getting Sober

I got sober, and three years later, met a man who also had three years of sobriety. He had been raised an atheist, but found that praying to God got and kept him sober.

Five years ago, when we bought our first house, we agreed to find a church. We never knew that The Salvation Army was a church, so we were surprised to see a sign at the corps near our house that said Worship Service Sunday at 11 a.m.

An Invitation

It was Christmas week. We got there at 10:55. We were standing in the back of the church when a woman there approached us and invited us in. (She had just changed her clothes for a sacred dance.) We went in and took a seat. The sacred dance was amazing. When I saw the love this woman had for God, I knew I was home. My husband grew to love the corps, but told me he would never wear a uniform. Within a year we became senior soldiers and have never looked back.

We are active doing things like ringing bells, serving food, helping with the toy shop and serving as assistant welcome sergeant.

God's Love

God never gave up on me, which I find amazing. At one time I had knowledge of God in my head, but now He lives in my heart. My life is so blessed. I have a God who answers prayer, loves us unconditionally, is always there and welcomes us back with open arms and when necessary puts a sign in front of a building. I would not have thought to look to the Army when I was looking for a church.

God has put people in my life like my corps officers who teach and challenge me, my Bible study group, my Sunday school, friends that I can laugh and cry with and a husband who loves me and loves the Lord.

Dorothy Sapp, a senior soldier, is the assistant welcome sergeant at the corps in Nashua, N.H.

A Betting Man
Wins the Pearl of Great Price

Competition and gambling played a tremendous role in my life at one point. In fact, I gambled my way to salvation.

Growing up in Spanish Town Jamaica and raised by my great grandmother, I learned all the good principles of life from her. Unfortunately, that life was short lived, for she passed away when I was about seven years old. My life took a turn for the worse after this.

I decided that I was going to figure out the rest of life on my

Lt. Kevin Bryan

own. My father had immigrated to the United States when I was three and I didn't know who my mother was.

I went to live with my aunt, but life with her was very difficult. I experienced more abuse than one can imagine. When I turned 13 I couldn't take it anymore and decided to run away.

Track Athlete

Life on my own proved even more difficult. Competition and gambling started to take over my life. I was a track athlete as far back as the first grade. Running was all I knew, and competing became the best outlet to get me through difficult days. Track team was becoming my chosen career path. I would race people for money outside of school as a means to survive. However, gambling led me to some compromising situations where I narrowly escaped with my life.

I eventually moved in with my father's mother, who did not have time to raise children. She didn't provide much guidance.

Real Winnings

Even though I had a guardian, I had no supervision and it felt as if I was raising myself. Then came the day when I made a bet that would change my life forever. I made a bet with a friend to set up a date for him with a girl from my school.

She was the daughter of the corps officer of The Salvation Army. The bet was simple! Set up the date and go to The Salvation Army on Sunday to collect the money.

In some situations I narrowly escaped with my life

I showed up at the corps that Sunday to collect my winnings and I left a born again believer. I surrendered my life to Christ that day, and I have never looked back.

I give all the glory and honor to God because in the midst of my desire to have life my way, God chose to have His way with me. He took me from where I had no direction and placed me on a path guided by His will. Now I am living for Him and am excited to see what He is going to do in my life in the days to come.

I am no longer a gambling man, but I can bet that God has great things in store to do and to discover.

Lieutenant Kevin Bryan was ordained and commissioned as a Salvation Army officer on June 6, 2010, in White Plains, NY.

Thanksgiving Turkeys
Gaining More Than We Gave

Jim and I are first generation Salvationists from the Antioch corps in northern California.

Jim and Dayna Carr

It happened when Jim heard a radio appeal, asking for donations of turkeys for Thanksgiving meals. Jim bought several turkeys and took them to the distribution center. The volunteer there asked him if he could take the turkeys to the church.

"Sure, which church do you want me to take them to?" Jim asked.

"The Salvation Army church," the volunteer said, to which Jim replied, "I didn't know The Salvation Army was a church."

At the corps, Jim met the officers, toured the building and picked up a brochure about the corps' worship services, activities and programs.

This all happened at a time when we were not attending a church regularly. Jim felt something missing in his life, and decided he would try this Salvation Army church.

Clap and Shout

Jim was apprehensive and at the same time strangely drawn by what he experienced. He had never been in a church where people clapped their hands and sang praise and worship songs. The quiet little church of his youth was just that, quiet. You sat in the pew, listened (and tried to stay awake) but you never yelled out "Amen!" or clapped your hands to the music. Jim continued to attend Holiness Meetings at The Salvation Army every Sunday.

Little by little, the Holy Spirit melted his heart until one day he accepted Jesus and was born again!

I thank the Lord for that day. You see, since then, our entire family has been changed.

Since that first call for turkeys, the Lord Jesus has been working in all our lives, changing us into new creatures. We have become soldiers. Jim, our daughter Wendy and I were made soldiers on the same day. Our oldest son, Tim, was blessed by serving on summer assignment in the Marshall Islands, where he felt the Lord call him to become a Salvation Army officer. He is now a captain, and was recently assigned to duty as the youth secretary in the Alaska division.

Our youngest son, Greg, has also been born again and although he has not felt God calling him to be a soldier, he occasionally attends the Army corps in Orlando.

What my husband first thought of as a call for turkeys was really not about turkeys at all. It was about Jesus calling us all to salvation and service.

Jim and Dayna Carr live in Sacramento, CA..

God Must Have Smiled
To See Me Wearing A Uniform!

I grew up in a suburb of Indianapolis, Indiana and had never seen a Salvation Army Christmas kettle until the day I happened to pass a Salvationist in full uniform ringing a bell. Continuing on my way to the technical school downtown that I was attending, I said to God, "Lord, they would never get me into one of those suits!"

Major Bruce Williams

Years later, while in the Navy, I was introduced to a very attractive young lady named Faith who happened to be a Salvationist. We fell in love and were married shortly after I was discharged.

Dance Hall Corps

Faith attended the Riverview Terrace Outpost in Tampa, Florida. You would never put this building on any poster to attract future officers. The room that we had services in was a dance hall on Saturday night. We had to carry our song books back and forth to the services because if we left them people would take them and try to sell them door to door. They would take our offering envelopes and use them to collect money as well. Because there was no air conditioning we kept four large sets of doors wide open.

Although it was as humble a corps setting as you could find, God's presence was always there. Seekers were drawn to the altar in every service.

Many times the seekers who came forward were the same as the week before, but their hearts were tender. Many people came from families that often needed to talk to God.

Kids a Handful

My plans were set as to how the next six years would run for Faith and myself. We would help out with the youth group for about two years and then be off to college on my G.I. Bill.

Those kids were a handful. Every Tuesday I came away

Major Williams receives Silver Star as his son Bruce, Jr., becomes an officer.

from the meeting vowing that I would not go back, and every Tuesday I went back. I began to notice how many doors the Army uniform opened for witnessing. The Lord began to break down my feelings about "that uniform." I joined The Salvation Army and put that uniform on. I was sworn in as a soldier a few days before Youth Councils were to be held. Faith and I then learned that we had been signed up for something called an FOF breakfast. I had no idea what that meant. When I was told it meant Future Officers Fellowship, I was really upset.

I had joined the Army, but being an officer was just not in my plans. Time went by and one day I realized that I was holding down a job because I had to eat, but I was ministering at the out-post because I loved it.

I was never struck by lightning or saw a vision, but in my heart of hearts I knew that God had chosen Faith and me to be officers. This June marks my 35 years of service. That day in December when I looked up and told the Lord, "That uniform is not for me," I believe He looked back at me and smiled.

Major Bruce Williams is a corps officer in Charleston, WV.

A Thrilling Ride
Not Knowing What Was In Store

It began with a report I had to prepare for a college class. I was attending Frederick Community College in Maryland. My plan was to complete two years there and then enlist in the military and continue my education later. Enlisting did not seem like a bad prospect since the Vietnam War was winding down and the military draft program had stopped the year before.

Little did I know what was in store for me or how my plans would change.

Major Michael Hawley

The assignment was to prepare a presentation on any subject I chose. We were to pick the topic, conduct the research and make the presentation to the class.

As I considered what to choose, I thought of the building I walked by almost every day—the Salvation Army Corps Community Center. All I knew was that the organization seemed to have a good reputation for helping people and that it was highly visible during the Christmas season. Beyond that, I had no clue.

Wearing my best blue jeans and t–shirt, my hair nearly down to my shoulders, I was granted an interview by the folks in charge, corps officers Captains Charles and Betty McClure. It was the beginning of a thrilling ride. My encounter with The Salvation Army on that day ended up taking me places over the next 30+ years I never thought I'd go, doing things I never thought I'd do with people I never thought I would be associated with.

Measuring Stick

My research took me to the Salvation Army corps hall where I attended Holiness Meetings, Salvation Meetings, Youth Meetings and Sunday school. Each one contained some teaching or sermon based on the Bible. I was told about my need for a Savior and

Majors Michael and Teresa Hawley on duty in Kuwait

that Jesus was the Savior. I had to wrestle with the concept of not comparing myself to others but of accepting the Word of God as my measuring stick. It led to me finding the condemning statement: "All have sinned and come short of the glory of God."

"All" included me.

Eternal Matters

It took a few months of prayer and preparation, but the corps officers and their assistant led me by their example and counsel to see that the Bible is the Word of God and not just an anthology of men's best writings, and that it speaks of eternal matters, not just temporal, and truths like who we are and where we're going.

At the end of a typical Sunday morning message, the invitation to come forward was given, and I knelt at the altar and gave my heart to Jesus. With that surrender came the readiness to commit to this organization, if there was a place to serve.

"It took me places I never thought I'd go"

That's where I still serve today.

Saul was serving his daddy by chasing donkeys when he met Samuel the prophet, who anointed him to be the first King of Israel.

Saul hadn't been just chasing donkeys. He had really been getting to the place where God would anoint him for a greater destiny.

I thought I was just visiting The Salvation Army to do a report for school, but God used that occasion to change my life, and generations to come as a result.

Hallelujah!

Majors Michael and Teresa Hawley, officers of the Southern Territory, are currently stationed in Kuwait.

Starving for a Change
Leaving the FastTrack Behind

I was a happy little seven–year–old ... before my parents divorced. My life was a whirlwind for a long time after that. We went from having everything to mom and me standing in welfare food lines.

My mom got jobs at restaurants. My dad remarried right away. Mom was an entertainer. She loved people, loved to sing and play the piano, and everyone loved her.

As a teenager I was on a fast track of self–destruction. There

Sandy Hall

were people in my life who didn't mind adding to that destruction. By 19, I'd had it with partying and took a hard look at myself. "If I were to die tomorrow," I thought, "no one would notice."

I resolved to change the way I was living. Easier said than done! I was around people who woke up every day just to figure out where their next beer would come from. I was tired of this life but didn't know where to go from there. But I knew if I didn't do something I would lose my mind.

Long Way From Peaceful

About a year later my dad called and asked if I would come to his house and talk to a minister. I couldn't believe my ears. My dad never talked about God—except when he was mad—so this was a big thing. I went to my dad's house in 1979 and met Pastor John from the Baptist church, who asked if I wanted to be born again.

This was all a surprise to me. This man looked like a big kid with wonderful eyes and a peaceful spirit, and I was a long way from being peaceful. We sat at my dad's kitchen table and I said the sinner's prayer.

We started attending the Bible study. I would listen hard and watch every move. I was starving for a change in my life, I was so unhappy. After a few months people stopped coming to Bible study, and I was back to square one. I knew I needed to have a quiet time, pray, have devotions, talk to God and let God guide me.

"What kept me from living like the Bible says?"

Things weren't working very well for me. I was still waking up around alcoholics and drug addicts. But I needed to keep trying. I found Pastor John at church and one day when I raised my hand for prayer, he called me to the front. I literally could not move out of my seat, I was so afraid. Pastor John walked toward me all the way to the back. He asked if I would speak with his wife who was also in the back. I looked at her and asked, "If I am born again, why is it that something keeps stopping me from living like the Bible says?"

She showed me John 8:36: "Those whom the Lord makes free shall be free indeed." I felt better and more confident. I knew I was on my way to a better life.

My Little People

During my search, the babies started coming. I had been with the children's father for six years. When they started they didn't stop. Every year another one, and then I said that's enough. When I was pregnant with Vanessa her dad went to prison for two years for possession of marijuana. When he got out I became pregnant with Jeremy and then Becky.

With so many children I started to go to The Salvation Army because it was within walking distance. Captain Hill was a single lady officer then. The corps was full and every seat was taken. But she took time to sit next to me and my kids. That meant a lot to me. One time the captain gave me a Bible for bringing the most people to Sunday school. They were just little people that I brought with me, so I was stunned that she did that.

I finally had the assurance that I belonged, and had found where my heart belongs.

When Christmas came I rang the bell at the kettle and brought in some good buckets! It took two days to thaw out.

Today I am remarried. I'm not a perfect Christian, but I do know one thing for sure. I love God and I thank Him for Jesus. I know the Army is my church, where I belong. I was recently commissioned Home League secretary and assisted in enrolling my daughter in Home League. My husband was enrolled as a Senior Soldier on Easter. God is good.

My dear precious mother, who passed away two years ago, is in heaven with Jesus and I know that I will see her again some day because of what the Lord has done in my life.

Sandy Hall is a local officer at the Salvation Army corps in Bay City, MI..

9 Adult Rehabilitation

"I will exalt you, O Lord, for you lifted
me out of the depths and did not let my
enemies gloat over me."

Psalm 30:1

Broken, But Restored
God Had to Drag Me Out of Abuse

When I am asked to give my Christian testimony, I usually start with my shoe. The bottom of it was how I felt when I walked into the Salvation Army Adult Rehabilitation Center (ARC) in Philadelphia back in 2000. It was no coincidence that I ended up there. It was divine intervention.

Madeline Bates

A Broken Life

My life up until that point had been nothing but broken.

I came from an average middle class home. We always had the necessities, and then some, but unfortunately my mother was very abusive and my home life was anything but average.

I was only allowed to go to school and come straight home; no friends, no social functions and constant beatings. I had no self–esteem.

Since abuse was so normal to me, I ended up in an abusive relationship and stayed for 11 years. I began drinking in order to cope and it became my crutch. I eventually left that abusive relationship, but I couldn't leave the alcohol. My life got progressively worse and I hit bottom.

God had to drag me through what I went through because He loved me so much that He did not want me to die without being saved. He kept showing me the way to His Son, but I refused to listen. It was only in brokenness that He brought me to my knees so I would finally look to Him for my answers.

Turning Point

The turning point in my life came when I was introduced to Christ as my Savior while I was at the ARC.

Seven months after I entered the ARC, I graduated from the program and was hired in the dispatch office. I was then promoted to resident supervisor and eventually I became a counselor. Later I was enrolled as a senior soldier (adult member) in the Army's church. The one person who had the most influence on me and who guided me in my Christian walk was Major Evie Wilson. Major Wilson is so spiritually grounded and such a good Christian woman that I really wanted to emulate her.

In 2004, I left the ARC to work as the office manager at the Salvation Army's Pioneer Corps in Philadelphia, the first corps in the nation! Then in December 2006, Major David Wilson gave me a call. He said he wanted me to come back to work at the ARC as the bookkeeper.

I just know that God has brought me back full circle to help me lead others to Him. I may be paid to be the bookkeeper, but my purpose is to share with others what has been freely given to me. It is one of the reasons why I was "volunteered" to teach the "Freedom in Christ" class.

"Freedom in Christ" is a class that allows me a chance to minister to virtually everyone who comes through the center.

I have no idea where God will take me next, but I know that I am here in the Army to stay.

Madeline Bates lives in Philadelphia, PA.

Grace and Freedom
From Prison to Ministry

I grew up in Racine, Wisconsin. I was raised in the Baptist church, ordained as a deacon, and served as church treasurer.

I earned a B.S. in Business Administration from Carroll College in 1977. After graduation I worked for Wisconsin Telephone Company in Milwaukee, Wisconsin. In 1984 I earned my M.A. in Communications from Marquette University.

After graduation I interned with Olgilvy & Mather Advertising in New York. In 1986, while working in sales for United Airlines in Chicago, I was transferred to Phoenix, where I started my own consulting business.

Lt. Willie Bland

Not having a personal relationship with Jesus Christ, I wandered away from the faith and as a result made some bad decisions. I tried to sell drugs to raise money for my consulting business. For this offense I was given five years probation.

Sentenced

The bad decisions continued. In 2001, after completing The Salvation Army Adult Rehabilitation Center (ARC) program in Phoenix and becoming assistant manager at one of the thrift stores, I relapsed.

As a result, I was on intense probation for exactly one day before absconding. Eight months later, when they caught me, the judge sentenced me to prison to complete the three and–a–half years that remained on my probation.

In July 2004, after completing a year and–a–half of my sentence, I was transferred to Winslow, Arizona. In Winslow I began to reflect on the idea that it was by God's grace that I was still alive despite my battle scars. God had been with me through it all.

So I decided that I would seek God and see if I could develop a personal relationship with Jesus Christ. I began to go to chapel services, started a devotional where I read my Bible daily and began praying that Jesus would come into my life.

New Life

God does answer prayers, and since Jesus has come into my life. I have experienced a wonderful change.

> "It was by God's grace that I was still alive . . . despite my battle scars"

I completed my prison sentence with no problem, and entered the Army's ARC in Phoenix clean and sober. For three and–a–half years I continued to work on strengthening my spiritual life.

I became an adherent, graduated from the program, began working for The Salvation Army, and became a soldier. I entered training to become an officer in The Salvation Army in August, 2008.

It is by the grace of Jesus Christ, the love of God and the fellowship of the Holy Spirit that my life is not what it used to be. In my service as an officer I look forward to carrying the message that Jesus can make you free on the inside as I render service to others in His name.

Lieutenant Willie Bland was ordained and commissioned as a Salvation Army officer on June 13, 2010 in Cerritos, CA.

God of Second Chances
Putting My Priorities In Order

You never know how God will intervene in your life, and how He will use certain circumstances to get your attention.

As the judge slowly lowered his gavel and sentenced me to complete a six month program at the Kansas City, Missouri Salvation Army Rehabilitation Center (ARC), I couldn't have imagined how God could use that moment to intervene and transform my life.

I was trapped in a world of self–neglect, self–destruction and addiction to alcohol. Before being

Lt. LeOtis Brooks

sentenced to the center, the only thing that I knew about The Salvation Army was the 15 second commerical clips that I occasionally saw during television sitcoms of someone donating their clothing to the thrift stores, and of course the Christmas bell–ringers.

Torn Apart

I entered the doors of the Adult Rehabilitation Center (ARC) on February 8, 2002. I was beaten down and torn apart by a world of darkness and despair. But within the confines of those walls I found, hope, life, forgiveness and a place that I could call home. I found out God loved me for who I am, in spite of my circumstances and all the things I had been through. He still loved me!

As the captain spoke one Sunday morning, it was as though he was speaking directly to me. When I walked down the aisle to accept Christ into my life, it was as though all of the pain and anguish I had been carrying inside was lifted. I was truly free!

After finding forgiveness and God's restoration, God used the officers, employees, and other residents at the ARC to help me learn how to become a better person, husband, father, son and friend. As a result, God gave me back my life and my family.

LeOtis Brooks and the Brooks Family

Shining Light

Deuteronomy 6:12 says, "Be careful that you do not forget the Lord, who brought you out of Egypt, out of the land of slavery." I have not forgotten that the Lord brought me through those tough times. God brought me out of my self–neglect and the bondage of addiction and gave me a second chance to live a life with purpose.

Now I have made the choice to make my family a high priority. I have decided to live my life for God. As a result of that decision, I entered the College for Officer Training in Chicago to become a Salvation Army officer. We will take our next step on that journey of second chances now that we have become officers.

Today God continues to place people in my life who offer spiritual support and guidance. They are my beacon of hope so God can use me to intervene in the lives of those who feel lost.

Through Christ, I have become a beacon of hope as He allows His light to shine through me, allowing others to see His light and find their own second chance.

Lieutenant LeOtis Brooks was ordained and commissioned as a Salvation Army officer on June 14, 2009 in Merrillville, IN.

Beyond Imagination
A Peace The World Cannot Give

I was blessed to come to know Christ during my first encounter with The Salvation Army. I was lost, empty, and full of despair in my struggle with drugs and alcohol. I had finally reached the end and I knew the last option was rehab or death.

A friend recommended the Army's Adult Rehabilitation Center (ARC) in Denver and I knew that it was my only hope. I remember being so afraid, but there was this indescribable peace I felt at the same time. It seemed as if God was holding my hand during this process, reassuring me that it was going to be all right.

Lt. Maggie Lopez

End the Pain!

One of the requirements of the program was to attend the Sunday worship at The Denver Red Shield. I immediately felt like part of the family. Captains Ron and Roberta McKinney made me feel so welcome and loved. I knew then that this was a place I wanted to be a part of. I came to the mercy seat with all my struggles, pain and burdens and laid them at the cross of our Lord and Savior. I was in so much pain when I knelt before God, and was ready to hand my life over to Him because I couldn't do it anymore. I didn't want to feel the pain anymore, I couldn't try to keep myself sober on my own anymore. I needed Him more than I had ever needed anything.

Amazing Experience

I had the most amazing experience that Sunday morning. God Himself came into my heart and saved me from a broken life without Him. My relationship with Christ has allowed me to do things never imagined.

Not long after I arrived at the Denver ARC, I met my wonderful husband and we were blessed with a beautiful and amazing little girl.

I never thought I would one day say I am serving the Lord through the work of The Salvation Army, let alone have a personal relationship with our Maker and Creator. It has been such a privilege to serve Him and to have Jesus Christ in my life. It's the best gift I could have ever imagined.

I wish I could say that it has been a trouble free journey. I wish I could say there aren't days when I throw my hands in the air and cry "Why God?" Those days still happen. But God has faithfully led me through some incredibly difficult journeys. I have been able to do such mighty things, all through the power of Jesus Christ.

To be willing to serve Jesus Christ, even when it doesn't make sense, is the ultimate blessing possible.

Lieutenant Maggie Lopez was ordained and commissioned as a Salvation Army officer on June 14, 2009 in Cerritos, CA.

Clean and Sober
Going the Distance

Facing a sentence of 25 years to life in prison for cocaine possession, Ricardo Manzano sat crying in a jail cell waiting to appear in court.

"I prayed in that moment that God would deliver me from this," Ricardo said.

An ex–gang member in his twenties entered the same cell and befriended Ricardo. Without hesitation, he shared with Ricardo about his life and about finding Christ. He shared Scripture with him as well.

Ricardo Manzano

When Ricardo stood before the judge on his day in court, he could only trust God. With great compassion, the judge decided that, because Ricardo had never harmed anyone but himself, he would not spend the rest of his life in prison. She sentenced him to five years and eight months.

As he stepped into the cell at Folsom State Prison, Ricardo encountered a guidebook to a new life. He found a copy of the *War Cry* on the floor.

He read in that issue about a man who had served time in state prison and how he became close to Jesus and found redemption. Ricardo soon decided he wanted that also and began writing to Salvation Army Adult Rehabilitation Centers (ARCs) across the country.

The ARC in Pasadena, California wrote back to him and for almost three years, Ricardo corresponded with an employee there.

On the day of his parole, Ricardo went straight to Pasadena.

While beneficiaries are required to be free from drug and alcohol for five days when entering an ARC program, Ricardo had been sober for five years while in prison. The intake worker asked why he thought he should be admitted.

"I knew I had to learn about this disease or I would go back to using all over again," Ricardo remembers. "I wanted a new life."

Ricardo was admitted and began the one–year program to recovery, but he found himself living out of a shopping cart on the streets following his graduation. Two months later, he entered the ARC program a second time and invested himself in it.

"I loved to visit the Army," he said of his Sunday mornings spent at Pasadena Tabernacle Corps. "The people opened up to me. I got to know them and they got to know me. I found a sponsor through the church, Jim Hennessey, who I still talk to and learn from."

Having lived on the streets, Ricardo now participates in the Saturday morning homeless breakfast feeding at a local park. He returns to the Pasadena ARC for an early Sunday morning service before attending worship at the corps, where he is now a soldier and plays in the brass band for worship. Ricardo recalls always wanting to be part of a choir and now he sings with the Pasadena Tabernacle Songsters. He has served as a songster now for two years. On New Year's Day for the last two years, he has marched down Colorado Boulevard, carrying a flag with The Salvation Army band and timbrels in the Rose Bowl Parade.

He works as a cook in a nearby alcohol treatment center and hopes to become a licensed alcohol and drug counselor.

"I feel so happy—like I'm on fire—when I come here," Ricardo says of the corps. "I know if I leave this place I would go back to using drugs. This is my strength, right here. This is where my new life started and continues."

Ricardo Manzano lives in Pasadena, CA.

No Plan of My Own
Pulled Through Open Doors

I met The Salvation Army through no plan of my own. I now know that it was God who brought me here.

I believed in Jesus when I was very young, but had lived most of my life in sin and separation from the Lord. After a breakup with my fiancé, I saw my life as over. I chose to look down instead of up.

I turned to what would become a continuance of an addiction to drugs instead of turning to the Lord. Next thing I

Kathleen Griffiths

knew it was 2004, I was turning 40, and I was sure that I had thrown my best years away. I had been masking my pain, stuck in a vicious cycle.

Love in Action

I knew I needed a miracle from God, but was also afraid of one. It came in the form of a minor possession charge and a couple of months in jail. I knew I needed to turn from my old ways. I was still so full of anger and self–pity. I prayed to God in my helplessness and He immediately began to open doors.

I began to follow, sometimes being pulled through! I prayed for a Christian program and the courts sent me to the Salvation Army San Francisco Adult Rehabilitation Center (ARC). I was thrilled to find that they had two Bible studies and two holiness meetings per week. I thought The Salvation Army had only thrift stores!

Here I witnessed Christian love in action through the Army officers in charge. I continued to open my heart to Jesus after 30 long
years. He welcomed me home like the loving father didfor his re-
bellious son in the story of the Prodigal Son.

After graduation, I
continued on at the Sal-
vation Army Harbor
Light Transitional
Program. I went back to
work as an employee at
the ARC. It was while
working there with
newcomers, volunteer-
ing to visit rest–homes,
and helping with home-
less outreach through
The Harbor Light that I

felt God's calling on my life to become a Salvation Army officer!

My Best Years

I have received the gift of salvation and been shown the gift of
recovery. I have no stronger desire than to share my faith and hope
with others, showing them that recovery and renewal are possible
through Christ Jesus. I live now for His purpose, soldiering at
Harbor Light and have gained experience as corps assistant for the
last two years. Here we are seven years later and my husband and
I are in training to become Salvation Army officers. God is showing me these are my best years, as I am living to joyfully serve Him
and others!

Kathleen Griffiths lives in San Francisco, CA.

Manning A Mission
An Epicenter of Help and Hope

Darrell Williamson is a man on a mission. He knows that the disease of addiction takes lives. And he knows with certainty that the Salvation Army Adult Rehabilitation Center (ARC) saves lives. He says, "Seven years ago I started a new life as a beneficiary in the Adult Rehabilitation Center in San Diego. I knew that people cared about me and my future life in sobriety. I completed the ARC program and left the ARC for a year, living a life of abstinence and renewal in God successfully.

Darrell Williamson

"I then came back to the ARC as a volunteer, wanting to give back. It was then I realized that I wanted to become a counselor like the people who had helped me in my recovery."

To do that, Darrell went back to college and earned his degree (where he had a straight A record and made the Dean's List) in addiction counseling and returned to the Salvation Army ARC as an Intern. He is now the lead counselor at the San Diego ARC.

"I truly feel I am doing the Lord's work," he says. "I'm giving back the love and compassion that was so freely given to me.

"Because of the encouragement of our staff, and the good people I have met while being part of this worthy cause, I am now a soldier (senior member of the church) in The Salvation Army. I have aspirations of one day becoming an officer and specializing in rehabilitation work."

As lead counselor, Darrell is part of a program that takes on some of the most difficult cases of alcoholism and drug addiction in the county. Darrell has a unique understanding of these people and their problems. He is

now an articulate, respected professional who reflects on his own odyssey from hopeless addict to solid citizen. After 34 years of drinking and drugging, and living on the streets and in prison, he made a decision for Christ that has transformed his life.

Darrell recalls vividly a sermon one Sunday that had the most profound impact on him. It was about Jesus' parable of the mustard seed. Its message of hope spoke to him and he believes the Holy Spirit came into his life that day and changed everything. He surrendered to God and then he pursued his recovery in earnest.

Today Darrell is lead counselor, intern trainer and re–entry coordinator for the rehabilitation program. He feels that because he is "one of them" he's particularly suited to this work. Captain Grady Brown, administrator at the San Diego Center, agrees. "With his professional expertise, and his own inspiring personal saga of salvation, he's an invaluable addition to our staff."

Darrell says that he could be the poster child for "before" and "after" drug use. Having endured stabbings, shootings, sickness, jail, homelessness and profound feelings of worthlessness, he says, "I was no good to anyone." His transformation into a healer and helper is all the more amazing.

—Marlene Gerber, who wrote this article, lives in San Diego, CA.

Darrell Williamson lives in San Diego, CA.

Mission Not Impossible
The Common Denominator at "Sally's"

Jim Bagwell is a man on a mission. He knows with certainty why "Sally's" is known as the "last house on the block." As the director of rehabilitation services at the Army's Adult Rehabilitation Center (ARC) in San Diego, he and his staff take on some of the most difficult cases of alcoholism and drug addiction you will see.

The sick and the desperate come through the doors seeking relief from lives of misery and despair. Their common denominator is loss—extreme

Jim Bagwell

loss. Jim understands. He has been there himself.

The men often come from the ranks of the homeless. Many have tried and failed at other programs. Some have exhausted resources at private rehab places. They're all ages, although more 30–somethings come now than in years past. They're from a surprising variety of ethnic and socio–economic backgrounds. They've lost everything—homes, jobs, family, health, insurance and hope. They have nowhere else to go… except "Sally's."

Bankrupt

After years of drinking and drugging, Jim too, had lost everything. His wife and children were long gone, as were jobs. He was financially and spiritually bankrupt. One night in 1989, while homeless and sleeping in the bushes in Balboa Park, he was attacked by knife–wielding thugs and left to die.

Jim realized he was "one sick puppy" and found his way to The Salvation Army and begged to be taken in. He went through many poignant and gripping experiences on the long journey back. A profound spiritual awakening proved to be a breakthrough in his recovery.

From the moment he arrived at the sprawling complex in downtown San Diego, Jim said he knew he was in "God's house." He surrendered to God "and I started talking to Jesus Christ. I know I wouldn't have made it without that."

Like those in his charge now, Jim lived there for six months, worked in the recycling warehouse and embarked on an intensive recovery program. He would get up when it was still dark out to go to work—sorting and tagging donated merchandise, repairing TV sets and radios, and taking breaks for counseling, chapel, 12–step meetings and meals. He was ready when donation trucks arrived to unload bunk beds and sofas. He would drop into bed bone weary each night. But it was the best he had felt in years, perhaps in a lifetime.

The holistic approach to recovery, he explains, is treating the mind, body, and spirit. Work therapy and a faith–based program, The Salvation Army knows, are the major components necessary for sustained recovery.

Jim's Test

Proof of Jim's recovery came one day in the bottom of a donation box he was sorting through. Hidden among drug paraphernalia and old clothes was a stack of $100 bills. Fighting the temptation to flee his hardships with this stash, he concluded that if anyone would ever trust him again, he had to do the right thing. He turned in the money.

While Sally's was "the last house on the block," it was definitely not the end of the road. Jim graduated in 1989 and entered Bridge House—the transitional living program. Since then, he's earned a college degree, established a successful career, and became a dedicated family man. He's come full circle.

"With his professional expertise, and his inspiring personal saga of salvation, he's an invaluable addition to our staff," says Major Oliver Stenvick, the ARC administrator.

"Thanks to The Salvation Army, and divine intervention, my life was saved," Jim marvels. "So I know the infinite possibilities of this place."

Now his mission is to guide others on the rocky road to recovery.

—Marlene Gerber, who wrote this article, lives in San Diego, CA.

Jim Bagwell lives in San Diego, CA.

10 Sunday School

"Start children off on the way they should go, and even when they are old they will t turn from it."

Proverbs 22:6

Eye On the Prize!
A Sunday School contest got my attention

I was born in Michigan in 1921. In 1927 our family pulled up roots and moved to California. After a year or so we moved to Santa Barbara. At that time I was seven years old.

My first contact with The Salvation Army was through one of my 5th grade classmates. There was a Sunday school contest, the prize being a bicycle for the boy or girl who brought the most people to Sunday school.

My classmate was the son of the corps sergeant major. They

Brigadier Betty Whiteside

lived across the street from the Army. My family lived a block away. This experience led me to get involved with youth activities and Sunday services at the Army.

Deciding for Christ

In 1934, when I was twelve years old, I was permitted to attend the youth councils. I was one of the many young people to make a decision for Christ that weekend. From this experience, I became part of the Corps Cadet program and other activities in the corps.

At the age of 16, I felt the calling of the Lord to become an officer. I finished high school at the age of 17 and, immediately following that, my application was accepted for the training college.

Early in the summer, the corps officer,

A fifth grade friend told me about it.

Major Frank Mann, was asked to tell me to wait a year because of my age. I entered the training college in September, 1940 in the "Crusader's" Session.

There were 24 people in the session. On April 1st of the final days of training we were told that we would be commissioned in May by General Evangeline Booth.

Assignments

For most of my career as an officer I served in the Booth Memorial programs for unwed pregnant teens. After 35 years I was appointed to divisional

Brigadier Betty Whiteside with her nephews—Edward Lemons, commander in the U.S. Navy Reserves and Jesse Calles, Sr., soldier at the Salvation Army Oxnard, CA corps.

headquarters in Los Angeles in various areas of service. In 1986, after more than 45 years, I retired and continued to serve for ten years in post–retirement as director of Senior Adult Ministries.

The journey with the Lord, serving in the Army, has been great!

Brigadier Betty Whiteside lives in Oxnard, CA.

Trailer Court Kids
Learning About God's Love

We were called "trailer court kids." My twin sister Yvonne and I, along with our three siblings, grew up poor. Dad had a drinking problem and couldn't keep a job for very long. I remember one time we needed shoes for school. Having no money, my mother went to the bank. The manager of the bank took my mother's driver's license as collateral and gave her money out of his own pocket for the shoes.

Yvette M. Dobney

We also moved a lot. That meant visiting many different churches, as we had no particular affiliation.

Wanting to Help

In one of the churches we met a teacher whose name was Michael. She treated us trailer court kids as if we were like any of the other kids in the class. She taught us that no matter who we are, God loves us. This act placed in my heart a deep desire to help the poor know Jesus.

I grew up, got married, had two sons—all seemed well. But it wasn't. I went through a divorce, moved with my sons to be near my family and enrolled in college.

After two years, I met a man named Gary who had gotten a job as a teacher in my small town in Wisconsin. We were soon dating, and Gary told me a lot about himself. He told me his church was The Salvation Army. I had no idea The Salvation Army was a church.

Gary and I became engaged and we visited his hometown in a suburb of Detroit. The boys and I met his wonderful family, and we attended the Dearborn Heights Citadel corps. As I sat beside Gary a warmth settled upon me as I realized this church was what I had been yearning for all my life.

Yvette as a child

Gary and I were later married. For 11 years we drove 600 miles each summer to visit family and to volunteer at the Army's Eastern Michigan divisional music camp. We involved ourselves in The Salvation Army as much as we could. I learned how the Army shares the love of God with everyone, and that it even gets down in the "trenches" to help the very poor. I enjoyed reading the book *The General Next To God*, which relates the inspiring story of William Booth, who founded The Salvation Army.

Now we drive an hour one way to the Eau Claire, Wisconsin corps with our four children. Gary is the song leader there. We have ordered our uniforms and we are taking classes to become soldiers. Finally I will wear a soldier's uniform! And finally I have found my "church" home—a place where the love of God dwells in the hearts of those who want to make a positive difference, a place to make a difference in the lives of those no one else would consider. Even us, the trailer court kids.

She taught us that no matter who we are, God loves us. This act placed in my heart a deep desire to help the poor know Jesus.

Yvette M. Dobney and her husband Gary accepted staff positions at the Army's Sierra del Mar Camp in southern California.

I Searched No Further
And Never Looked Back

The only thing that I knew about The Salvation Army was that once every six months they came to our small town, conducted an open–air meeting, and then took collections. My mother often told me what good people they were.

Major Juanita Clevett and her husband, Major R. Ernest Clevett.

Mink Farm

In April, 1951 my mother and father packed up the car and my brother and I for a "long trip" to Lynnwood, Washington. My mother's aunt and uncle lived there and fortunately had a place for us to stay in exchange for helping them with their mink farm. We remained there throughout most of the summer. During those summer months I would walk to all of the churches that were near our home and attend their Sunday school and morning worship service. I did not find any that seemed to fill my need to grow in my Christian walk.

Just before school was to start that fall we moved again to a house south of Everett, Washington. I again searched for a church that I could call *my* church. The first week of school I met a lovely Christian girl named Betty. She invited me to attend a service at The Salvation Army. I first went to their YPL (Young Peoples' Legion) which was held every Friday night at the Everett corps. It was there that I immediately felt right at home and knew the Lord had placed Betty there for me. To this day we still communicate with each other regularly.

I searched no further, spending as much time there as I could and still keeping up with school and homework. In January, 1952, I was enrolled as a senior soldier of the Everett, Washington corps. I was active in the Girl Guards, Corps Cadets and Young People's Legion, as well as taking up collections at local bars, etc.

Youth Councils

It was at a Youth Councils in Spokane, Washington, that I felt the Lord's call to officership (full time pastor) in the Salvation Army. A chorus tells the rest of my story: "I've never been sorry I heeded God's call. I've never been sorry I gave Him my all. My walk with the Master grows sweeter each day. I've never been sorry one step of the way."

My husband (Captain Howard William Birks) and I served in corps, Harbor Light and ARC appointments prior to his death in November, 1991. I remained in that corps appointment for nearly two years more, at which time I

I knew the Lord had placed Betty there for me.

was assigned to THQ in the officers' sick benefit department. Two years later I took early retirement in order to marry my present husband, Major R. Ernest Clevett, who had already retired. In these past 12 years we have taken several post–retirement assignments in both the Southern and Western territories. The Lord has blessed me beyond measure! Praise His name!

Majors R. Ernest and Juanita Clevett live in Coeur d'Alene, ID..

Getting Serious With God
Awestruck by His Power

Before accepting Christ I began attending Sunday morning church services with friends. My family didn't attend. I believed in a "higher power" and I thought that was enough. I didn't know it then, but God's grace was evident many times when I was saved from awful situations. A few years after high school I married Dan and we began to toy with the idea of our family going to church.

Captain Amy Voss

Playing at Church

At age 21, pregnant with our second child, I accepted Christ and my life began to change. We moved to Michigan's Upper Peninsula and had our third child, but only played at church. We were not yet serious in our relationship with God.

We had hard times in our marriage. At one point I even moved back with my mom for a few months. Our friends prayed for our marriage. After a few months Dan and I were back together and our fourth child arrived. We realized then that we were ready to get serious with God.

We found some friends from years ago who attended the Wesleyan church. That church had closed but Glen and Mary were attending The Salvation Army, so we thought we'd try it. There we began to grow in the Lord.

Following Christ faithfully began at The Salvation Army where our children attended the character building youth programs. I grew in Christ as we attended Sunday school, Holiness meetings, Salvation meetings and Bible studies.

Camp

I had a crash course in the "Army" one summer when I worked at Little Pine Island Camp in Grand Rapids, Michigan. My calling to officership was

Captain Amy Voss, husband Dan and children Lorena, Danny, Andrea and Cameron.

slower than my husband's. One day when we toured the College for Officer Training in Chicago, I said, "I could live here."

We have had many challenges coming to training. God worked miracles and moved mountains to get us here. I'm in awe of what God can do. I used to put limitations on God and He would exceed them. I put my life and my children's lives in His hands. He knows the plans for us. It is all for our good.

As I take this step into officership, I will have great opportunities to live my life for Him. I'm scared and it has not always been easy to follow Christ. At times I may feel like I'm in the unknown, but when I have that chance to turn and look at where He has brought me I rejoice and take another step with Him.

Captain Amy Voss is a Salvation Army corps officer in Sault Ste. Marie, MI.

A Landlady's Love
Striking A Deal for the Kingdom

Whenever somebody asks me where I attend church, my answer—"The Salvation Army"—always evokes the same response. "I didn't know it was a church." I have been a member for 50 years. How did I come to know about The Salvation Army?

When I was six weeks old my family moved into a rental bungalow. No hot water or bathtub; but there was a river that ran through what was to be our backyard. The landlady lived in a large house next door and she always kept an eye on us.

Major Marilyn Aldridge

Her mother was a member of The Salvation Army. The summer before I started school we attended a two–week vacation Bible school there. We loved it! Just before Labor Day our landlady made an offer that got my mother's attention. She told my mom it was time to raise the rent, but if my parents could see their way clear to let my brother and me attend Sunday school she said she would try to hold the rent down. They made the deal. That is how we became faithful attendees in their church, The Salvation Army.

We weren't allowed to be sick or miss Sunday school for any other reason during the next seven years. The rent remained the same. My brother enjoyed the summer camps and youth groups. I seemed to flourish in the drama opportunities.

The summer we entered junior high school we moved into a new home. Now my parents were ready to expose me to "real" churches. I attended them with my cousins and neighbors. I just wasn't comfortable in those situations. The message was the same and I wasn't confused in my beliefs, but there was just something about The Salvation Army I missed. The people were happy and they treated me like I was special.

During all of this time I was being subjected to abuse at home. My secret! At home I was told I was bad, and at church I was told that God loved me. By then I felt a desire to pursue becoming a Salvation Army officer. It meant that I would need to attend the Army's training college in Chicago for two years and be ordained. I knew this would meet with opposition from my mom, but I failed to consider God's power in every situation. He had a plan. I was about to see Him in action.

A new captain was assigned to Niles, Michigan where we lived. I became the babysitter for their three girls. One day the captain approached me about entering a speech contest. I had to write a speech to go along with a chosen theme, then deliver it. My mom had to sign the application and refused to because she was sure I was going to make a fool of myself. I prepared and prayed that I would be good enough to win third place, but I won first place.

Our captain worked it out that my parents could go with us for the finals in Chicago. They were actually walking on the campus where I wanted to study for ministry. As I stood before thousands of people and gave my speech that evening, I was proud that my parents were there. I didn't win that night, but I was a winner. God opened a door and my way was made clear to go to the college for officer's training, where I was ordained in 1965.

My husband, three children and I served people in need for 40 years, until we had to retire early because of illness. My parents eventually joined The Salvation Army and became very active.

Come to think of it, that landlady struck a pretty good deal for the Kingdom of God.

Major Marilyn Aldridge is now retired and living with her husband, Major Robert Aldridge, in Sioux Falls, SD.

I Said "No" to the Army
Until I Saw the Big Picture

I didn't know that The Salvation Army was an actual church until my parents announced to my brother and me that we were going to attend a church service there. My family had been looking for a new church for a while after leaving another denomination that held many false beliefs about Jesus, His birth and His life. I had no idea what to expect from the Army on that chilly Sunday in March.

Audrey Hickman

Meeting Debbie

When we walked in the doors of the Oakbrook Terrace, Il corps we were greeted by a rather loud and cheerful woman in a navy blue uniform we would later come to love as Debbie. She showed my family and me to the chapel for the Sunday school opening; we sat down and listened.

During the 10 or 15 minutes that it lasted, word had spread of my family's arrival. Exiting the chapel door, I was greeted by three girls and a woman in one of those navy blue uniforms with a "Hello Audrey. My name is ... Nice to meet you," but I hadn't even introduced myself. I had no time to think of how they learned my name as they led me to Sunday school.

As we walked into the classroom the teachers introduced themselves to me and I sat down. I kept wondering, "Why was everyone wearing those navy blue uniforms?" Everyone in Sunday school seemed really close, like they were family.

We were invited to stay for lunch but declined, as my mother
was a bit overwhelmed by all the friendliness and those navy blue
uniforms everyone was wearing. I thought the church was all
right, but I didn't want my parents to choose The Salvation Army
for our church home.

Angry at God

Later that summer my parents told us that The Salvation Army
was, indeed, our home church. I was angry and upset with that
decision. I told them that I was never going to wear that uniform.

As summer turned to fall, youth activities started up and I
began to attend the various meetings and retreats. A year later I
became the first soldier in my family to proudly wear the navy
blue uniform. Through corps events and teen activities I have
gained most, if not all, of my closest friends.

I remember how mad I was at God when my family joined the
Army. I see the bigger picture now and understand the reasons why
my parents decided to join. Most importantly, I have grown
tremendously in my faith and spiritual walk since I entered the doors
of Oakbrook Terrace corps. Thank you Lord for Your wonderful
plan for me!

"Be joyful in hope, patient in affliction, faithful in prayer" (Rom.
12:12).

Audrey Hickman is a soldier at the Oakbrook Terrace corps in Oakbrook, IL.

Girl From Tway Holler
Kentucky Corps Officer Comes Knocking

I was from the "coal camp," and I spent my first memorable days in Tway Holler, Harlan, Ky. Had the Harlan corps officer not "come knocking on our door" we may never have ever met The Salvation Army.

We only went to town every other week on Saturday mornings. On the way to "town" we stopped for gas, my brother and I got a moon pie and an RC cola to share, and then we went to the dime store, the A&P (for things the commissary didn't sell) and

Major Sherrie Klemanski

then back home. I know about "mountain" people and their ways.

Mountain Roll Call

My mother, after learning about the Army, used to go into people's houses up in the hollers, pull their kids out of bed, wash and dress them and send them out to the church bus. The corps officer's wife was doing the same thing. It must have taken the corps officer two hours each Sunday just to get everyone on the bus.

Within a year of meeting the Army, Mom was running two outposts (very unofficially for years), conducting Sunday schools and Home Leagues. Mom would often return to the homes and cook meals, bathe the children and their sick mothers and mend clothing. On one or two occasions she prepared the dead for burial. She even scrubbed their floors with lye soap—but I had no idea why until I read the book *Smoky Mountain High* by Major Frank

Duracher (Crest Books 2007).

My mother dressed in her uniform, bonnet and all, every Saturday morning. The corps officer picked us up, took us back to the building where he took care of us all day, gave us lunch and assigned chores even to the smallest child. My chore was to scrub the toilets and empty the trash cans. I had to be taught how to clean the toilet bowl because at home we did not have one and I was too little to put the lye in the outhouse.

Legendary Dedication

Mrs. Captain Buttler drove the ladies throughout the county "collecting with their tambourines." (Captains Carlton and Elizabeth Buttler provided me a solid foundation for who I am today. My mother said Mrs. Captain Buttler never said an unkind word to anyone.) It was once said that my mother would

> **"We only went to town every other week on Saturday mornings"**

go down into a ditch beneath a utility pole until the worker would come down and give her a quarter and take the *War Cry*. That was the kind of dedication it took in the mountains, and the kind of love that made our Sunday school attendance run in the hundreds.

When the mining was depleted in Tway, Kitts, Gray's Knob and a few other places, The Salvation Army closed up and left town. That was in 1959. My parents moved us to Covington, Kentucky. Mom worked at the Salvation Army's Booth Hospital there for 14 years. It was her first "paying" job. I became a Northerner with a Southern heart.

Smoky Mountain High was on several of my Christmas gift lists last year. When some of my Kentucky Baptist family get to read it, hopefully they will understand why my mother and I felt the call to minister through The Salvation Army.

My husband, Frank, and I have just completed 40 years of service and will each have given 48 years at the time of our retirement, if the Lord allows.

One story of Salvation Army service I heard from Brigadier Doris McQuay was about a mountain missionary who ran out of gas and walked to the general store for some. The apologetic storekeeper said he had sold his last gas can and he had nothing to transport it in. The missionary lady spotted an enamel bedpan and she said, "that will do." She filled it with gasoline and walked back to her jeep. As she was pouring it from the bedpan into the gas tank, a fellow came along and yelled, "God bless you Ma'am, I wish I had the kind of faith you have."

Major Sherrie B. Klemanski is a retired officer.

Refuge for a Hurting Teen
"They Let Me Be a Kid"

I wasn't sure. I didn't know anything about this Salvation Army and I needed to find out. Since I was only eight, I ran home to my mother. "Can I go to church? The Salvation Army church?"

My mom seemed to know a little more than me and said, "On the white bus?"

"Yes, it'll be here soon. Can I go?"

My mom stood with us as we waited for the bus to come. I still remember when it turned the corner to our street. I noticed for the first time the red shield on the side

Lt. Nicole Ross

as it pulled up to the sidewalk. My friend and I were on our way.

Instant Embrace

I attended Sunbeams that afternoon ... and began my lifelong love for The Salvation Army. I might have been the new kid that day at Sunbeams, but I never felt like one. I was instantly a part of the group, instantly embraced.

Years passed and I found myself not attending just Sunbeams but Junior Soldiers, Songsters, Sunday school and church. I loved every minute of it. It was a wonderful place. The more programs I was introduced to, the more I fell in love with the Army.

The Army was a place of love, acceptance and patience. Quickly it became my sanctuary, the place I wanted to be more than home.

The Lord would also bring a godly man into my life nine years later who I would date and marry.

Can I be a kid?

Home became a bit chaotic in my early teens, as my family struggled to overcome the grip of addiction. I did not want to struggle through it. I just wanted to hide from it. I wanted to be where life seemed easier, where I could just be a child. I did not want to have to worry so much. The Salvation Army was the place where those desires became a reality. They were hard years and, to be honest, I was not the easiest teenager to deal with, but it did not seem to make a difference to anyone at the Army.

Still Loved

Then my life was rocked when the corps officers (my pastors) were transferred. They were the only officers I had ever known. How could this be happening? I needed them.

When the new officers arrived, I was angry. Even so, they eagerly accepted and embraced me. No matter how difficult or angry I was, I was loved at The Salvation Army. And I discovered that the new officers weren't so bad after all.

While attending my first Youth Councils, I felt for the first time that I needed to pray. Then I needed to cry. I cried out to the Lord. I knew He wanted my life; He wanted me to let Jesus live in my heart. I prayed and I was saved! But I did not want to go home. Although I was different, home would not be. But I did have the assurance that God would go with me no matter what might happen.

I changed that day. Things did not magically get better. We still had to work hard to be the family we are today. But God's saving grace is sustaining, bringing light in the darkness. So instead of being angry, I became hopeful, hopeful for God's restoration.

God however, was not done with me. I felt a stirring in my heart a few months later while attending Labor Day camp meetings. It was in response to a call to officership.

You mean me?

I argued with God. I told Him "No, this is crazy. I can't do it. I

am too weak, too broken, there has to be someone better than me."
Once I stopped arguing with God and myself, I found to my
amazement that I was standing up in front of the whole camp
meeting to testify that I was called to be an officer.

Twelve years have passed since God first called me. The road
has been long, but God has been faithful.

I am so grateful for that big Salvation Army bus, and I thank
God for it. I am His vessel, ready to do, go and be whatever the
Lord may require of me.

Maybe there are other little girls who need to take a ride on a
big Salvation Army bus, just like I did.

Lieutenant Nicole Ross is a Salvation Army corps officer in Plymouth, MA.

11 Musical Gifts

"Praise the Lord with the harp; make music
to Him on the ten–stringed lyre."

Psalm 33:2

A Great Neighbor
And the Blizzard of 1978

Early in our marriage in 1966 we were a young, growing family with twin daughters. We bought our first home near the railroad tracks in the center of our town. I was a 23–year–old firefighter working 24–hour shifts. My wife Marianne was a busy stay–at–home mom. We struggled financially, as most young families do on one income.

Marianne met a wonderful neighbor lady, Gen Madsen, who was looking for someone to clean her home. She worked as a church

John Baldus and his wife Marianne

secretary while also caring for her family. Marianne and I discussed this opportunity to supplement our income and how Marianne would be able to take our twins along when cleaning this lady's house. Later we found out they were Salvationists and her husband Walter was the CSM.

Army Friends

That was our first contact with the Army. Over the next few years our contact with the Army was spotty. Occasionally I was asked to put on programs for the Home League and youth groups on first–aid and safety in my capacity as a firefighter.

Marianne's friendship with Gen and her husband grew. We continued our involvement with our own church, where we served as Sunday school teachers, choir members and deacon.

Memorable Morning

Then one memorable Sunday morning in 1978 our city of Grand Haven in western Michigan was hit with an unusually heavy snowfall and blizzard. We awoke and began getting ready for church. I looked out the window and all I could see of our car was the radio antenna sticking out of the snow. Our local radio station was giving out all the church closings.

Our three children (son Carl was the youngest) were excited as they thought we would be staying home and they could play in the snow. Mom and dad had other thoughts. We had decided to walk to the nearest church one block away. We all had fun walking through the deep snow and drifts. When we arrived at the church, Marianne said, "You know, The Salvation Army is only one block further," so we pushed on and attended the service at the corps.

Coming Home

I enjoyed the brass band and Marianne liked the smaller church feel. It reminded her of the small rural Baptist church she attended in childhood. We occasionally began to visit the corps and open–air meetings in the summer months. The corps sergeant major frequently would ask me to join the band. He knew I had played the trombone in my school years.

Active Service

Eventually, in 1982 we became senior soldiers of the corps and also served as bandsmen at the corps and divisional levels, and as Sunday school teachers, missionary sergeant, Home League and League of Mercy members, timbrelist and songsters. Marianne has been on two short–term missionary trips to Jamaica and St. Martin. In our retirement years we remain active in the corps.

We feel blessed to have met the Army and to serve our Lord and Savior Jesus Christ.

John C. and Marianne Baldus live in Grand Haven, MI.

My Written Invitation
Singing and Praising God

I was born in Yorkshire, England, and lived with my mother. When I was about five years old I started going to the Church of England Sunday school with some neighbor children. I always came home singing the songs and choruses I had heard that day. After a few weeks I brought home a note to my mother: "We feel it would be advisable to keep Molly home another year or so as she disrupts the class by clapping for every song." My mother was amazed. When she asked me why I clapped, I told her because it felt good. So, the matter rested for a while.

Molly Laxton

Pestering Mom

One Saturday we found a postcard had been pushed through the letterbox. It read, "IF YOUR CHILD DOES NOT ATTEND SUNDAY SCHOOL, SEND HER TO THE SALVATION ARMY." Oh, I was so excited, but my mother was very hesitant and only said "yes" after I had pestered her a while. But she had no intention of getting up early on Sunday morning. She worked very hard as a head cook in the only hotel in the area, and Sunday was her only day off.

Sunday morning I was up early, washed, dressed and had breakfast before I woke my mother. When she realized I REALLY wanted to go to the Army, she got up and walked me over to the corps and asked what time she could pick me up. Afterward we walked home singing and clapping all the way. I went there for several weeks, and was encouraged to sing and clap. I was at home!

No Problem!

We moved to another town, and as we were moving in a neighbor came over to welcome us. During the conversation she asked my mother if I went to Sunday school, and my mother told her we had yet

Molly Laxton and family.

to find The Salvation Army. The neighbor laughed, saying, "Oh, that is no problem, I am the Home League secretary there."

God was certainly paving the way for me.

I became a junior soldier and loved that corps, where there were lots of young people. I sang in the Singing Company, fell in love with the nicest boy in the Young People's band, and several years later became his bride. We have two wonderful daughters and six beloved grandchildren.

This year we celebrated our 58th wedding anniversary, and we are living happily ever after in Clearwater, Florida. My husband still plays in the band, and I am the Home League chaplain.

God is good.

Molly Laxton lives in Clearwater, FL.

A Message in the Music
Fantasia Lyrics Pierced My Heart

"Join the Salvation Army and See the World" is inscribed on one of my tee shirts. That phrase has meant more and more to me as I've grown in the Army for the past 20 years.

My father, a fourth generation Mormon, played trombone in his youth. Following my father's musical example, when I was nine I also took up the trombone.

When I was a kid, prior to meeting the Army, I happened to tune into a TV program that featured a Salvation Army Songster

Dennis Sibley

Brigade in stand–up collar uniforms. They were performing Christmas carols. I remember asking myself, "Who are these people?"

A Musical Introduction

Later in high school, a biology teacher of mine just happened to mention that he gave to The Salvation Army because of a positive experience he had with the Army in his time of need. One of the students mentioned, "But they wear those funny clothes!" In my junior year, a fellow high school band student, Maury Priest, showed me his silver trombone. He mentioned he played in a Salvation Army Band and invited me to come to his corps band rehearsal.

Impressed with his musical talent and because of my two previous exposures to the Army, I went to the rehearsal with my trombone to check out those people dressed in the funny clothes!

Upon Bandmaster Gordon Damant's downbeat I heard glorious

sounds coming out of the cornet section of the Sacramento Citadel Band. One of the band members was the notable Eric Loveless. Another was Erik Sholin. At that instant I was hooked on the sound of the Salvation Army Band. From that time forward I would shuttle back and forth between my Mormon ward meetings of priesthood, Sunday school, and Sacrament meetings and

Sacramento Citadel Band engagements at Holiness services, Open–Air Meetings and Salvation Services.

Christ Is the Answer

During my association with the Sacramento Citadel Band I was introduced to recordings of the Hollywood Tabernacle, Oakland Citadel and International Staff Bands. I copied one long–playing record, The Holy War, onto a reel–to–reel recording tape. That recording tape would later be my only connection with the Army. On that recording was Ray Steadman–Allen's "Fantasia for Pianoforte and Band." During an interlude in that song, the International Staff Band sings, "Christ is the answer to my every need, Christ is the answer, He is my friend indeed."

Many years later, when I was married and raising a Mormon family, the words of the fantasia kept assaulting my heart. After many years, those words finally pierced my stubborn heart. I asked Jesus to come into my life. Today, I am a student of biblical Christianity, an Army soldier and a member of the Tustin Ranch Salvation Army Band. I indeed see the world through opened spiritual eyes!

Once lost, almost found, lost and found again! Praises to Him!

Dennis Sibley worships at the Tustin Ranch, CA corps, where he is a soldier and a bandsman.

A Fruitful Night Shift
Putting Time to Good Use

Wes Sonnier got more than he bargained for when he answered a help–wanted ad in a newspaper in Lake Charles, Louisiana. His response to a job opening as the night desk man at The Salvation Army's Center of Hope eventually led to a new direction in his Christian walk. Wes describes it as "totally unexpected and life–changing."

Wes Sonnier

Sharpening His Skills

The job description listed the need for someone to supervise the shelter during the "graveyard shift," from about 11 p.m. to 8 a.m. Wes got the job and found that during the wee hours of the morning there was usually not much to do. So he would practice his piano skills on an old upright stored just off the dining room.

"It turns out this guy is an accomplished pianist!" says Captain David Sams, corps officer. "Someone heard him playing one night and told me, since he knew our corps desperately needed a piano player."

A Music Ministry

Captain Sams approached Wes about playing for corps worship services and Wes quickly agreed. The more Wes learned of the Army's mission and doctrine, the more he fell in love with his newfound ministry. In fact, his wife of 34 years, Sharon, began faithfully attending as well.

Wes and Sharon Sonnier were recently enrolled as soldiers of the Lake Charles Corps. They proudly wear their uniforms and are faithful in helping the corps family in its discipleship efforts.

God's Plan

"I thought the Lord was through using me because of some low points in my life," Wes Sonnier testified. "But all of that changed when a classified ad in the paper led to my answering the Lord's calling to become a Salvationist!"

—Major Frank Duracher is the author of this article.

Wes Sonnier is a soldier in Lake Charles, LA.

My Second Life
Back to the Band

I met The Salvation Army very late in life. I was 75 years old when I became a soldier.

In my first life, as I generally refer to it, I was a musician. I played trumpet in a symphony orchestra (many of my colleagues in the Seattle Temple Band would find that hard to believe), gave lessons and worked for whoever called me.

In my second life I was involved in special education. I taught children with disabilities, obtained a doctorate in that field

Tom Lovitt

and was employed as a professor at the University of Washington. I was there for 35 years.

During the years in education I played my trumpet only occasionally. My wife, when engaged as a public school music teacher and later as a church choir director, scheduled me to perform with her groups, mostly at Christmas and Easter.

Since my retirement from the university I have volunteered as a court advocate for children who have been abused or neglected. I also assist first grade children at my neighborhood elementary school. In addition, I have collaborated with Casey Family Programs, a Seattle organization dedicated to assisting foster youth.

Can I Sit In?

In 2005 I attended a brass band festival in Bellevue, Washington. I was so impressed that I wanted to be a part of one. Three of the bands were from the Seattle area. One was the Seattle Temple Band. I read the list of personnel of the three bands and it was obvious that several families were represented in the Salvation Army group. That appealed to me. I called Stefan Wennstig, the bandmaster, to ask if I could sit in at a rehearsal. He said that would be fine. The next day I rented a cornet and showed up for a rehearsal. I did my best to keep up but I was totally bushed at the end of the 90–minute rehearsal. I had not played in an instrumental group in more than 40 years.

"In my first life ... I was a musician."

I Was In!

I never formally auditioned for the band, but I was gradually accepted. After a few weeks the librarian assigned me a locker in the band room and gave me a name tag to put on my cornet case. A short time later the bandmaster allowed me to take a folder home to practice. He then invited my wife and me to the annual band and songsters picnic. After a few more weeks I was included on the band's e–mail list. I figured I was in!

I didn't expect the level of spirituality shown by the Seattle Temple group. A prayer is given before the band plays for the Sunday service and band members offer devotionals on rehearsal nights. In my early days I had performed with several musical groups, but prayer was never a part of their routines. I thoroughly enjoy playing with the Seattle Temple Band—there is nothing like the sound of a brass band—but the fellowship among the group is the most meaningful part. Regularly, a half dozen or so band members at each service or rehearsal ask about me or my wife or others in my family.

New Soldier

After 10 months of participating and after taking classes to learn more about the Army, I was enrolled as a soldier. The mission of the Army is amazing and I am blessed to be a part of it. I have collaborated with a few Army members on tutoring programs and shared ideas with others about helping foster children. I hope to serve the Army in more ways, preferably in line with my experiences with children, especially those with special needs.

Tom Lovitt is a soldier in Seattle, WA.

Coming Home
Choosing to Honor My Gifts

I was born into the Jewish faith, but I was never comfortable within its structure. Something was missing in my life. I did believe in God, but yet I felt that God wanted more of me than just believing in Him.

Joel Vogel

Bottomless Cup

When I was young, God gave me wonderful gifts. I never thought of them as gifts from God, but I loved these gifts for the exhilaration they gave me. In high school I played on the baseball team and learned to play the cello.

I was awarded a scholarship to the school of music at the University of Colorado in Denver. But I had also received a letter from the New York Yankees, inviting me to attend a tryout. I played in AA baseball for two–and–a–half years, but a severe knee injury cut my baseball career short.

God also gave me prosperity in business for many years. Still he was not yet finished with my growing toward Him. After perhaps a lifetime, God knew that it was time to come to Jesus Christ and to Him.

Our nephew, who lived in Boise, Idaho, was constantly calling me to discuss baseball, football, or any sport. He was always telling us about Boise's beauty and how much we would enjoy living there. I always answered that it snowed in Boise and that I had forgotten how to wear snow boots. Before we moved to

Atlanta briefly to help my son and his family, we gave the nephew my son's phone number.

"Then I heard a loud voice. "Enough! This is where you belong!"

One day my nephew called and, as usual, told us how wonderful it was to live in Boise—and why didn't we come there instead of moving back to Florida. My wife was in favor of this, so off to Boise we went.

Once again, God was guiding my life. Not too long after we arrived in Boise, my wife and I found employment with The Salvation Army. One day we were driving around to acclimate ourselves to the surroundings and happened upon the Boise corps building. My wife told me that, when she was a child, her whole family attended the Salvation Army church in Albany, NY. She wanted to attend a service the following Sunday. Now God was drawing me nearer to Him.

Hearing God

On Sunday, we went to church. Upon entering, my wife stayed in the vestibule, speaking with the corps officer. I was drawn to the chapel. I felt I had to go in to seek peace. I sat in a pew and looked up at the cross—and a feeling of peace came over me. Then I heard a loud voice. God spoke to me, saying "Enough! This is where you belong!" I looked around, but no one was in the chapel but me. Then I heard these words again, even louder. This time, I knew it had to be the Lord. I listened intently, and at the end of the service, I would not leave my seat. After all, God had said that "This is where I belong!"

God had spoken to me! Never in my life had I heard such a powerful voice utter such powerful words, and yet sound so loving. The captain finally quieted me down enough for me to leave and I went home. We began to attend the church every Sunday. I constantly asked the corps officer, Captain Tom Petersen, question after question about Jesus and Christianity. Every question was answered with honesty and caring. I began to read the New Testament and found joy in what I read.

On Fire

One day, Captain Petersen came to my home to counsel my wife, about a problem. She went outside for a few minutes. Suddenly I became so hot and began to sweat profusely. The Holy Spirit had come to me. I began to scream at Captain Petersen that I needed to take Jesus as my Lord and Savior right then. Captain Petersen brought me peacefully to my Lord and Savior. What a wonderful day that was! To think that God actually wanted me!

God never stopped me from using the gifts He gave me. I have played drums in the corps band. I am also involved with the Adult Rehabilitation Program (ARP)—it has become my ministry. This is why God wanted me—to bring Him and my Savior to these men.

When Tom Petersen, then a major, was transferred to Reno, Nevada, my wife and I followed. My ministry is still here. I teach adult Bible study. I still play in the small band, although it's with an accordion. Most of all, I still love and help the men in the ARP. God gave me this soldiership and I wear the uniform of The Salvation Army humbly.

Joel Vogel is a soldier at the Salvation Army corps in Reno, NV.

Life Beyond TV Land
"I Had No Idea What a Christian Was"

Bob Casey has gone from being a rising young TV star to the life of an alcoholic to becoming a total–abstinence, uniform–wearing Salvation Army soldier.

Born in 1927, in Rochester, New York, Bob's father wanted him to follow in his footsteps as an engineer. But Bob had other ideas. He was bitten by the show biz bug and never recovered. Following two years in the U.S. Navy during the Second World War and graduating with a degree in drama from Carnegie Technical Institute, Bob set out to establish himself as a leading man.

Bob Casey

Trademark Lines

In the early days of TV it was common to try to bring hit radio series to the small screen. One such show to make the transition was the extremely popular comedy "Henry Aldrich." Two generations knew the trademark lines "Henreee, Henry Aldrich!" "Coming, Mother" and "Gee Whittakers, Homer, how is everything going?" But the stars who made the characters so memorable could not work in TV. Bob Casey at 22 was a perfect fit for the role of Henry Aldrich.

It was challenging work because in those days all television was live—no chance for retakes or covering mistakes. Catapulted to early fame, Bob was on his way to a high profile career as an actor.

McCarthyism

The paranoia of Senator Eugene McCarthy and his allies in reaction to the advances made by communism around the world convinced many that communists were undermining American society. Actors, writers, producers and directors were black-balled arbitrarily. Bob reported for his first day of the new season only to learn that he and another actor were fired. No reason was given.

Out of work in New York, Bob left to try his luck in Hollywood. But the movie industry was reeling, both from the McCarthy activity and the onset of television. After some roles in the TV series "Dragnet," Bob made his way back to New York and went into advertising.

At 22, Bob was a perfect fit for Henry Aldrich

Greater Setbacks

Along the way Bob suffered even greater setbacks. His only son was killed in an auto accident. His wife died suddenly. And Bob became an alcoholic. He could feel himself sinking. "I had no interest in religion," he recalls. "Oh, I dabbled in the philosophy of religion but I had no idea what a Christian really was. I knew I was missing something."

Finally, Bob joined Alcoholics Anonymous and found sobriety.

Eventually Bob remarried and moved to Florida. His wife, Trish, had attended The Salvation Army when she was younger but had not been to the Army in many years. One day Trish said she needed to be around people. Remembering her earlier days, she suggested that they go to The Salvation Army for church.

"I didn't even know The Salvation Army was a church," Bob says. "I had contact with the Army when I was in the service and stayed the night with them in Chicago. I donated to the kettles, but that was the sum total of my knowledge."

When the Caseys walked through the door at the corps in St. Petersburg, Florida, they were greeted warmly. Bob was immediately asked if he played an instrument. He admitted to playing cornet and minutes later found himself on the platform playing with the band.

The welcome touched him profoundly. "This was the first time I had come in contact with people who claimed to be Christians and were clearly living differently than other people I knew," Bob says. "I wanted what they had." Finally one Sunday he made his way forward to kneel at the mercy seat at the end of the meeting and accepted Christ as Savior.

In May 2008 Bob and Trish Casey were enrolled as Salvation Army soldiers. "The best thing that ever happened to me was finding The Salvation Army. It changed my life," Bob says, smiling.

—Major Allen Satterlee wrote this article.

Bob and Trish Casey are soldiers at the Salvation Army corps in St. Petersburg, FL.

It Happened In Brooklyn
A Beautiful Drummer Caught My Eye

On July 6, 1939 at the corner of 43rd Street and Eighth Avenue in Brooklyn, I came face to face with The Salvation Army for the first time in my 15 years of life. What caught my attention was the sound and appearance of about 25 people, most of them young, making music on a variety of instruments. They wore a uniform unfamiliar to me, the men in visored caps and the women in bonnets that looked like something from another age.

Arthur I. Anderson

The band sounded good so I stuck around to catch their act.

The music stopped and some of the instrumentalists talked about "what God had done for them in their lives." Then a young man came forward and opened a black book and began to talk about God and "His Son, Jesus Christ." I listened, but by this time my heart had been impaled by the drumsticks carried in the hand of the most gorgeous girl I had ever seen in my whole life.

The open–air meeting ended and the group packed up to go back to wherever they had come from. Having lost my tongue as well as my heart to this young drummer, I turned around and started for home. I hadn't gone far when I heard a high–pitched cry behind me. Turning, I saw the girl yelling to me.

She Noticed Me

She poured words at me like a torrential rain. She said she had noticed me in the ring. Noticed me? Wow! She saw I was interested. And how! She thought I might like knowing more about the group she was in and what they were doing. What I wanted to know more about was her and, so far, I hadn't even gotten her name. Would I "like to go with her to the Army this Sunday?" I almost dropped! Somehow, I got my mouth unzipped and said I would go with her anywhere. She looked at me funny, but her smile came back as she realized she had made more of an impression on me than she had intended. She said, "Meet me on that corner" and she pointed to a place a half block away.

That Sunday I waited on the designated corner. I didn't know that it was the corner on which the Army building stood. All of the signs were in Finnish, since this part of Brooklyn was a completely Scandinavian settlement. I'd assumed the building was a funeral home.

I was there ahead of time because I didn't want to miss seeing the girl of my dreams. People were going into the building, many in their funny uniforms. Then out she stepped. "Hi!" she said, smiling at me, "you made it. Come on in."

Trying to be cool, and gurgling some utterance of recognition, I stepped into the packed meeting hall. The band was on the platform. Others were in front with guitars. A lady at the piano played some music and the people in the audience were singing words I couldn't understand.

Strange Meeting

It was a strange meeting, but it was exhilarating. The songs were fast and done with a lot of hand clapping. The girl, who by now had gotten me into a seat, had taken her place in the band and was busy beating out the message. She looked at me two or three times while everything was going on.

A man and a woman were both leading the meeting, one in Finnish, the other in Swedish and English. The band played a march and I listened, entranced. When they finished, the string band took up the beat and carried on. Next, a soloist with a guitar.

After that a cornet solo by the leader of the band.

When all the music–making was over, the man in the gray uniform spoke in Finnish and his wife, who spoke seven languages, gave the sermon in Swedish, which was then translated into English by the lady at the piano.

There was an invitation to come to the altar, more choruses were sung, and then, an electric thing happened! Some of the people got up and started marching around the hall, grabbing flags and beating tambourines ... What I didn't know at the time was that this was a Hallelujah Windup! One by one more people left their seats, leaving me the only observer of this whirlwind indoor parade. When it all died down I finally determined that I wanted to be a part of this group because what they were doing was exciting. Everyone looked as if they were having the greatest time of their lives.

When the final prayer was said I managed to walk my dream girl home. She lived just a block away. I learned her name was Martha. She lived in an apartment with her mother, father and a younger sister. They were Norwegian and had lived in Brooklyn for most of their lives.

Martha and I became good friends. Soon I also became a part of that marvelous crowd of young people, and I became a soldier of The Salvation Army at the Brooklyn Eight Avenue corps.

Oh yeah, I also joined the band ...

Arthur I. Anderson is a soldier at the Salvation Army corps in Old Orchard Beach, ME.

12 Employment

"May the favor of the Lord our God rest upon us;
establish the work of our hands for us."

Psalm 90:17

Beyond Grief and Loss
In Place of Misery – Hope and Peace

Throughout childhood my life appeared perfect and I had no need for God. My life was shattered when my father was diagnosed with cancer. He was my hero. I could not imagine why God would allow this to happen to me. Two–and–a–half years later, my father passed away. My family really struggled with this.

Lt. Jennifer Masango

Grief and Loss

I became depressed and just hoped the sadness would go away. I was only 10 when my dad died and by the age of 12, I had determined that life stinks and the only way out of the misery was through death. I remember thinking that suicide probably wasn't the answer, but I was just so hopeless.

Over the next couple of years I refused to look to God for help. Then when I was 15 my mother was diagnosed with cancer. I could not imagine the grief of losing another parent.

One night I got on my knees and cried out to God. I was desperate. I said "Lord, if you are there … can you help me! Come into my life and make me a new person!"

I was on my knees weeping when I experienced hope for the first time. A peace that cannot be explained came over me. God had heard me, and I tell people that the Holy Spirit came to live inside of me that day and made me a new person.

Never The Same

From that day on, my life has never been the same! Thankfully, my mom did survive the cancer, but after that experience I knew that nothing was impossible with God. I learned that God is faithful to get me through anything that may come my way. His hope and peace sustain me in the midst of life's storms.

Lt. Jennifer Masango and family

Eternal Living

Since then, God has been in the process of transforming me. I attended a Baptist church for a few years and in 2000, I heard about a Salvation Army camp called Camp Gifford in Eastern Washington. I worked there for five years and loved the ministry of the Army. This was my first experience with the Army and where I began to feel God's call to full–time ministry.

I met my husband, Emmanuel, at this camp and he also felt called to ministry. By the time we got married we knew that God was leading us to be officers in The Salvation Army. Now, we are excited to see how God will continue to transform us and use us for His purposes and glory.

Thankfully, Jesus will be there to lead us in His service and we hope to be used in a mighty way for His Kingdom. Indeed, God does change lives! May we be His faithful servants and help change other lives for Him.

Lieutenant Jennifer Masango is a Salvation Army corps officer in Tualatin Valley, OR..

A Brush With Death
Turned My Life Right Side Up

I was raised with Christian values but wandered away from them in my teenage years in boarding school because I wanted to blend in with my peers. In 1988, a near death experience brought me some sober reflection. "If I had died, where would I have gone, heaven or hell?" This question never left me.

One day a nurse gave me a tract entitled "How To Have Peace With God." My simple prayer after reading it was "Lord, if you can save me, I will live all the way for you."

Captain Bayode Agbaje

Surrender

I accepted the Lord into my life. A heartfelt joy flooded my soul. I had an inward confidence, and with a resolute mind I surrendered all. This surrender included changing the friends I hung out with, reading my Bible and praying every day, joining a campus Christian fellowship and attending several weekly church meetings. I had a deep desire for more of God.

I graduated with a bachelor's degree in mechanical engineering in 1992 and served as a minister in the church while doing secular work. I worked as a plant engineer for the British Oxygen Company in Lagos, Nigeria until 1996, when I felt that God was calling me to a full–time ministry.

I had the opportunity to pastor four churches, including one that

I pioneered. I also took some
mission trips to assist with
the HIV & AIDS campaign
efforts in The Salvation Army
and to complete training
in child evangelism, world
missions and comprehensive
ministerial training.

In 2001, I became acquainted
with the Cleveland Adult
Rehabilitation Center and
learned of its need for a resident chaplain. I came to the U. S. to
serve in this capacity in 2003.

As a chaplain, I was fully immersed in center life. I shared the
Gospel with every beneficiary that came through the center. To
God's glory, many of them got saved and others rededicated their
lives to Christ. I am still in touch with some of them.

I am thankful for the opportunity to receive training in chemical
dependency and drug abuse counseling. One day, while looking
down from my apartment on a group of beneficiaries, I thought
about how the devil had robbed these guys of their lives. Moved
with compassion, I wept inconsolably, then I started sensing that
God was calling me to a deeper commitment in the Army. He
wanted me to become an officer.

I remember telling Major Cranford afterwards, "If the Salvation
Army is not doing God's work, who is?" He affirmed me in my calling.

I don't know what lies ahead, but I trust in the Lord who has
brought me this far. I am looking forward to a glorious fulfillment
of His plans in my future ministry.

Proverbs 4:18 says, "But the path of the just is like the shining
sun, that shines ever brighter unto the perfect day" (NKJV).

Captain Bayode Agbaje serves at the ARC in Cleveland, OH.

My Plans Slipped Away
After Summer Camp and Ground Zero

Growing up in England, I am sure I had heard about The Salvation Army, but I certainly did not know what it was or what it did. When I became a Christian at age 18, I attended a church that was just 500 feet from the local corps, but I was still unaware.

Captain Jon–Phil Winter

Camp

One year I decided to come to America and work on a summer camp staff at Camp Keystone in Florida. I enjoyed a great summer and returned for the next few years. Each summer I learned a little bit more about The Salvation Army, but I never thought of joining its ranks. Even when I moved to America to work full time for the Army I had no intentions of becoming a soldier, in fact I think I may have even used the word "never."

Ground Zero

Then the events of 9/11 occurred. I had the opportunity to volunteer at Ground Zero where I saw what a powerful impact The Salvation Army uniform had on the people working there. During the following Youth Councils, I remember asking God to show where He wanted me. I still had no desire to become a soldier, let alone an officer.

It was then that I felt the Lord asking me to notice where I was. I was standing in a sea of uniforms, and everyone around me was a soldier or an officer. I had never really run from a calling to be an officer, but I had closed my mind to the very possibility. At that moment I opened myself up to the calling and accepted it immediately. All other plans I had for my life slipped away and I suddenly felt a great peace about my future.

A Part of the Family

For me, joining The Salvation Army meant joining an incredibly large family. For a first generation Salvationist, this can sometimes be a little intimidating, especially when I think of those who have a long and rich Army heritage. But then I remember, William Booth was a first generation Salvationist too.

Captain Jon–Phil Winter is a corps officer in Chattanooga, TN.

Faith Wasn't Easy
Until the Army Saw My Potential

I was getting over a meth addiction and learning how to be a mother at the same time. I was working part-time at a local university and felt I needed a change. I didn't have a relationship with the Lord, but He was at work in me. I would think about church off and on, but I never went.

Tai Leathers

I had a very rough childhood. I grew up in inner–city projects and began dealing drugs to support my family when I was in junior high. It was hard to believe in God with all that I had been through. I guess I was a bit upset with Him in all honesty. Faith did not come easy.

My parents were drug dealers and addicts and they never took me to church. When I did go I felt like it was just a fashion show and I was being judged. Being discontent with where I was in life, I actually broke down and prayed—something I never did. I cried and I prayed, asking the Lord to help me understand what I should do with my life.

The next day a co–worker told me about a social work position opening at The Salvation Army in Fargo. I was reluctant to apply because I felt insecure and under–qualified. The pay was good, the benefits were great and I would be working with a population that I could relate to and longed to serve. With gentle nudging, I applied. I was offered the job shortly after.

Life Change

Working at the Army has changed my life, and you may even say saved my life. It provided me with everyday opportunities to see the Lord at work. The mission and the ministry of the Army let me see that there is still a body of believers that can bring hope for communities like mine.

It was a church willing to embrace it all, with Heart to God and Hand to Man. It was a church willing to reach into the depths of despair with a beacon of hope, without judgment. The work of the Army also gave me faith that I can make a difference in the lives of the people I grew up with. I pray every day that the Lord will use me to touch lives.

I started attending the Army's church in Fargo and accepted Jesus Christ as my personal Lord and Savior. Captains Deannie and Adam Moore are so faithful and obedient. The love of God shines through them and you feel it. They live in faith and inspire me to believe God has a plan for my life.

I was amazed with the acceptance I felt from the congregation. It was the first church I ever attended that did not make me feel judged. The people are very diverse and actually admit they are humans and have faults. The emphasis is not on who you are but who you have the potential to be in Christ.

One day my dad came to the Army and served lunch for the first time. I am praying that he will begin attending church. As the Family Services Director, I have special opportunity to interact with folks. Last month, while meeting with a client, I felt led by the Holy Spirit to pray with her. I said, "Lord, if you want me to do this I have faith you will give me the words" and offered to pray with her. She accepted. Later, she sent me a card saying, "I know there is a God when there are still people like you around." It meant the world to me. I keep it in my office to remind me that I can be used by the Lord to share the message of hope and grace.

Tai Leathers lives in Fargo, ND.

The Spirit Took Hold
Of My Self–Pity and Despair

I met The Salvation Army before I had accepted Jesus Christ as my Lord and Savior. My family had been given assistance by The Salvation Army many times over the years, but I never realized back then that it was a church.

Dave Beals

My first real contact with the Army came four years ago when I found myself unemployed. I answered an ad for bell ringers and was surprised to find out that the Army center had a chapel and that, in addition to its aid services, Sunday services were offered.

Not Religious

We were told that it was okay to say "God bless you" and "Merry Christmas" because The Salvation Army was a Christian organization. Even though I wasn't religious, I decided to do the best job I could and that included using those expressions. After saying "God bless you" a few times, I was surprised to realize that I actually meant it!

The real story isn't just how I met The Salvation Army, but why it was so important to me.

My First Fifty

I had spent my first fifty years living only for myself and never really giving any thought to who God was or what my relationship with Him was or should be. For most of those years, I felt like something was missing in my life—like I had a big gaping hole somewhere deep inside of me. I tried to fill that hole with alcohol, drugs and other pleasures of the flesh, but with no success. I wallowed deeper and deeper into self–pity and despair.

Then my life came crashing down to a new low. It wasn't the abuse of drugs and alcohol that did it, but two health problems combined to finish the job I had already started with my self–involved lifestyle. I thank God that I found Jesus in my life at the same time I was experiencing these health problems. Without Him, I wouldn't have been able to survive. I had The Salvation Army to thank as well.

> **I had a big gaping hole somewhere deep inside of me.**

Support

I first met Captain Tom Mason during the Christmas season four years ago. It was his example and encouragement that led me to begin reading the Bible for the first time in my life. I was absolutely stunned when I read Mark and Acts and learned firsthand about our Lord and Savior. Then I found myself in church on Christmas Day and felt the Holy Spirit take hold of me and lead me to accept Jesus Christ as my Lord and Savior.

My wife and I began attending services at The Salvation Army here in Dubuque, Iowa around Christmas three years ago and have been regulars ever since. We were both enrolled as soldiers in September of 2008, thanks to the encouragement and love we received from Captains Tom and Kay Mason, our corps officers and pastors. I hope to continue to learn and grow as a Christian under their fine leadership. God bless them both, and God bless The Salvation Army!

Dave Beals lives in Dubuque, IA.

Christ Filled My Heart
I'm Living Out the Gospel

While living in a high rise in St. Paul, Minnesota, I was talking on the phone to my friend who lived in another high rise and worked in a local restaurant in St. Paul. He had gotten involved in a dispute at the restaurant and told me he had decided to terminate his employment and to go to work for The Salvation Army as a bell ringer. He invited me to try this job option as well.

This was just a chance conversation and invitation that I didn't pay a lot of attention to initially,

Patrick A. O'Dougherty

but later I took up my friend's invitation to try ringing the bell for The Salvation Army.

Filling the Void

I had a very positive experience with the initial Sunday services I went to at The Salvation Army with Major Doug Yeck and Captain John Joyner. They helped me fill the empty spot of loneliness I had in my life. I found I could replace it with the presence of Christ. When I went to the first service, I felt at home. The Salvation Army does what many other religions talk about. "Let us not love in word, neither in tongue; but in deed and in truth" (1 John 3:18). This is the lived–out message of the Salvation Army.

In 2008 I went on a single's retreat at the Army's camp near Finlayson, Minnesota. The theme of the retreat was, "We are not owners of our time. Christ is coming again and He will break the hands of all clocks into infinity."

Borrowed Clothes

The Salvation Army retreat master, Sherri Trucker, led me into an accounting of my talents. I have spiritual talents like writing and music which I apply in song. I have income and inheritance which I have never been able to  let go of easily until now. I came to realize during the retreat that my talents are not my own. They are like borrowed clothes. I heard Christ call out "Get out of yourself" and heard the Angels singing "Holy, Holy, and Holy."

I affirmed at this retreat that the purpose of my life is to glorify God. The Salvation Army retreat was a life changing conversion of the heart for me.

On the way back to St. Paul, once again I was thrown into God's depths. I began praying daily. I began living a life of confession. I was truly transformed by conversion.

Patrick A. O'Dougherty is a member of the Army's Eastside Corps in St. Paul, MN.

Complete Surrender
Of a Cornet Player from Georgia

My calling as a Christian came before I was 12 years old, but it wasn't until just a few years ago that my life completely and utterly belonged to God and I accepted His calling.

My wife and I had established ourselves in Savannah, Georgia and developed some close friendships with other couples from our local church. This perfect life was turned upside down when I took a job with The Salvation Army.

At first, I felt that I was living well within the parameters of God's will with my social services position.

Lt. Preston Lewis

How arrogant was my thinking? I now understand that if I subscribe to the title of Christian, it means to completely surrender to the calling of the Holy Spirit. I made the first in a succession of decisions; I attended my first Salvation Army holiness meeting.

A Church Time Forgot?

I distinctly recall seeing the brass band and my snide mental comment, "a brass band, talk about the church time forgot." From this, I learned two things; first, God listens in on our private thoughts and second, He has a remarkable sense of humor because it seemed like I blinked my eyes and I was in uniform with a shiny new cornet tucked under my arm!

Initially, there was a tug on my heart, small at first, and I tried to dismiss it. It wasn't long before I felt the full weight of my calling to officership—and it was overwhelming!

After working for The Salvation Army for two years, I questioned my impact on those I was serving. Doubt began to fill my mind and I wondered, "Was I really needed?"

"We Need You!"

God answered that question early one morning when a frantic employee ran to my office and informed me that one of the shelter residents was in labor. Then she yelled, "She's having the baby now, we need you!" Immediately, I thought—I know the process takes hours and this cannot be happening because I'm the least qualified person in the building for this job.

I found the woman lying on the floor and, if that wasn't bad enough, the baby's head had been crowned for some time.

The woman calmed down immediately when she saw me, perhaps thinking this man with the pinstriped shirt and tie was a doctor. As the baby delivered, I discovered the umbilical cord twisted around her neck. I knelt there with a little baby girl in my hands who showed no signs of life and feared she was stillborn. I silently prayed, "Lord, this could be such an opportunity to show others just how wonderful you are, please don't let this baby die."

Those few minutes seemed like an eternity. When nothing happened, I began to pray out loud, "in the name of Jesus, breathe!" Immediately a small air bubble came from her nose and she let out the very faintest of cries.

Today, she is three years old and perfectly healthy.

How does this play into my calling? It was on this day that God answered my question, "Was I really needed?" Today, I am convinced beyond any doubt that I am following God's voice. He has certainly not disappointed me and I am committed to honoring Him through my service to The Salvation Army!

Lieutenant Preston Lewis is a corps officer in Ft. Walton Beach, FL.

No Longer Lonely
My "Coincidences" Were Part of God's Plan

After a long struggle with alcohol and drug addiction, my children were taken by Child Protective Services and my parents got temporary custody of them. I attended an in–patient rehabilitative program over 400 miles from my hometown and my family. When I finished the rehab, I moved into a Transitional Living Center to have a better chance at remaining clean and sober. These were state funded programs with no Christian emphasis whatsoever.

Misty Raup

Although I had turned my life over to God during this ordeal, I still felt very scared and lonely. I prayed for the Lord to keep me strong for my children and to ease my pain and loneliness. Soon after, a group of other believers in the halfway house reached out to me and we began supporting each other with Bible study and prayer each night.

One of these ladies directed me to the local Salvation Army Thrift Store. She had a clothing voucher to get items for her job search. I went with her, also searching for employment while we were out and about.

When we got there we were informed that their Family Services worker had left for another job. I informed the staff that I had some college training and management experience and that I was looking for work. (For a long time I was what you call a "functioning addict.") The officer in charge invited me into the office where I explained that I was a born-again Christian and had just made a commitment to the Lord to change my sinful ways and live for Him. I told him I understood if he did not want to hire me due to my sketchy past, but I would be willing to volunteer and do some office work until I found gainful employment.

He took my resumé and all weekend long I prayed my references would pan out.

Accepted

The following Monday I received a call and I was invited for a real interview, where I learned that The Salvation Army is much more than bell ringers, red kettles and thrift stores. How exciting it was to get the job! To think I could become part of this movement of ministry and social services!

I soon started attending the Army's worship services and became enthralled and amazed by the ministry, their doctrines, uniforms, and ceremonies. I knew within a month that I had found my church home. Nowhere else had I been fully accepted and loved as at The Salvation Army. Soon thereafter, I took a position as the acting Home League Secretary and six months later I was enrolled as a soldier.

Many other good things happened in my life. My children were returned to me and I was introduced to a wonderful Christian man. His first Holiness Meeting at the Army was the day of my soldier enrollment and he soon became involved in the corps and enrolled as a soldier (senior church member). We were married the same year and he is the proud father to "our" children.

Every Mother's Day is a reminder to me of what blessings I have received by God's grace.

A series of what some may call "random coincidences" were not only miracles, they were a part of God's plan for me.

As long as we keep Jesus first and in the center of our lives, things always work out.

Misty Raup is a soldier at the Salvation Army corps in Billings, MT.

Crest Books

Salvation Army National Publications

Crest Books, a division of The Salvation Army's National Publications department, was established in 1997 so contemporary Salvationist voices could be captured and bound in enduring form for future generations, to serve as witnesses to the continuing force and mission of the Army.

Shaw Clifton, *Never the Same Again: Encouragement for new and not–so–new Christians*, 1997

Compilation, *Christmas Through the Years: A War Cry Treasury*, 1997

William Francis, *Celebrate the Feasts of the Lord: The Christian Heritage of the Sacred Jewish Festivals,* 1998

Marlene Chase, *Pictures from the Word*, 1998

Joe Noland, *A Little Greatness*, 1998

Lyell M. Rader, *Romance & Dynamite: Essays on Science & the Nature of Faith*, 1998

Shaw Clifton, *Who Are These Salvationists? An Analysis for the 21st Century*, 1999

Compilation, *Easter Through the Years: A War Cry Treasury*, 1999

Terry Camsey, *Slightly Off Center! Growth Principles to Thaw Frozen Paradigms*, 2000

Philip Needham, *He Who Laughed First: Delighting in a Holy God,* (in collaboration with Beacon Hill Press, Kansas City), 2000

Henry Gariepy, ed., *A Salvationist Treasury: 365 Devotional Meditations from the Classics to the Contemporary*, 2000

Marlene Chase, *Our God Comes: And Will Not Be Silent*, 2001

A. Kenneth Wilson, *Fractured Parables: And Other Tales to Lighten the Heart and Quicken the Spirit*, 2001

Carroll Ferguson Hunt, *If Two Shall Agree* (in collaboration with Beacon Hill Press, Kansas City), 2001

John C. Izzard, *Pen of Flame: The Life and Poetry of Catherine Baird*, 2002

Henry Gariepy, *Andy Miller: A Legend and a Legacy*, 2002

A Word in Season: A Collection of Short Stories, (compilation), 2002

R. David Rightmire, *Sanctified Sanity: The Life and Teaching of Samuel Logan Brengle*, 2003

Chick Yuill, *Leadership on the Axis of Change*, 2003

Living Portraits Speaking Still: A Collection of Bible Studies, 2004

A. Kenneth Wilson, *The First Dysfunctional Family: A Modern Guide to the Book of Genesis*, 2004

Allen Satterlee, *Turning Points: How The Salvation Army Found a Different Path*, 2004

David Laeger, *Shadow and Substance: The Tabernacle of the Human Heart*, 2005

Check Yee, *Good Morning China*, 2005

Marlene Chase, *Beside Still Waters: Great Prayers of the Bible for Today*, 2005

Roger J. Green, *The Life & Ministry of William Booth* (in collaboration with Abingdon Press, Nashville), 2006

Norman H. Murdoch, *Soldiers of the Cross: Susie Swift and David Lamb*, 2006

Henry Gariepy, *Israel L. Gaither: Man with a Mission*, 2006

R.G. Moyles (ed.), *I Knew William Booth*, 2007

John Larsson, *Saying Yes to Life*, 2007

Frank Duracher, *Smoky Mountain High*, 2007

R.G. Moyles, *Come Join Our Army*, 2008

Ken Elliott, *The Girl Who Invaded America: The Odyssey Of Eliza Shirley*, 2008

Ed Forster, *101 Everyday Sayings From the Bible*, 2008

Harry Williams, *An Army Needs An Ambulance Corps: A History of The Salvation Army's Medical Services*, 2009

Judith Brown and Christine Poff, (Eds.), *No Longer Missing: Compelling True Stories from The Salvation Army's Missing Persons Ministry*, 2009 (compilation)

Quotes of the Past & Present, A Compilation from the *War Cry*, 2009

Henry Gariepy and Stephen Court, *Hallmarks of The Salvation Army*, 2010

John Cheydleur and Ed Forster (Eds.), *Every Sober Day Is a Miracle*, 2010

R.G. Moyles, *William Booth in America: Six Visits 1886 - 1907*, 2010

Shaw Clifton, *Selected Writings: Volume 1, 1974-1999; Volume 2, 2000-2010*, 2011

All titles by Crest Books can be purchased online at www.shop.salvationarmy.org or through your nearest Salvation Army Supplies and Purchasing department:

ATLANTA, GA —(800) 786-7372

DES PLAINES, IL —(800) 937-8896

LONG BEACH, CA—(800) 937-8896

WEST NYACK, NY—(800) 488-4882